TREES TIME ARCHITECTURE

Design in Constant Transformation

Andjelka Badnjar, Kristina Pujkilović, Ferdinand Ludwig, Andres Lepik (eds.)

PARK BOOKS A.M.

4	Foreword	**TO THE TREES!** Andres Lepik and Andjelka Badnjar
10	Curators' statement	**TREES, TIME, ARCHITECTURE!** Ferdinand Ludwig and Kristina Pujkilović
18	Essay	**TREE FUTURES** How Past Ideas Can Foster a Plant-Friendly Urban Future Sonja Dümpelmann
28	Drawing essay	**TREES FOLLOW DRAWINGS, DRAWINGS FOLLOW TREES** Noël van Dooren
38	Making as research	**US EASTERN WOODLANDS ASH, TAKE CARE** Jana VanderGoot with Kelly Church, Samantha Jamero, Shelbi Nahwilet Meissner and Rico Newman
44	Microhistory	**SHINING HOURS** Women Climbing Trees Tell a Story of Emancipation in Anonymous Photography Laura Leonelli
50	Photo documentary	**THIS LAND IS MY LAND** A Photographic Journey Through the Xylella Epidemic in Puglia Jean-Marc Caimi and Valentina Piccinni
62	Interview	**THE STATE OF LIVING ROOT BRIDGES IN MEGHALAYA TODAY** Morningstar Khongthaw and Wilfrid Middleton in Conversation with Kristina Pujkilović
70	Making as research	**DESIGN – BUILD – GROW MEGHALAYA** Combining Vernacular and Modern Knowledge Through Making a Living Root Pavilion Wilfrid Middleton, Zijing Deng, Elahe Mahdavi, and Ferdinand Ludwig
76	Memoir	**BOTANIC ARCHITECTURE** A Genealogy Mark Primack
86	Design practice	**MY ENGAGEMENT WITH GREEN ARCHITECTURE** Édouard François
92	Historical review	**LIVING IN TREES? A THOUSAND-YEAR HISTORY** Roberta Martufi
100	Film	**A TREE IS NOT JUST A TREE** Making the Film *Taming the Garden* Salomé Jashi
110	Interview	**TREES AND TIMBER** A Life Cycle Perspective Hannes Harter and Michael Vollmer in Conversation with Ferdinand Ludwig and Kristina Pujkilović
116	Design practice	**THE MAKING OF LIVING ARCHITECTURE** How to Design with Trees and Time Ferdinand Ludwig, Daniel Schönle, and Jakob Rauscher
122	Appendix	Biographies, Image Credits, Imprint, Acknowledgements

Fig 1 Primitive hut with allegorical figure of Architecture, engraving by Charles Eisen. Frontispiece of Marc-Antoine Laugier, *Essai sur l'architecture*, 1753.

Andres Lepik and Andjelka Badnjar

TO THE TREES!

Twelve-year-old Cosimo Piovasco di Rondò, the hero of Italo Calvino's novel *The Baron of the Trees*, climbs up into a holm oak in protest against his family. What begins as a spontaneous act of resistance turns into a life-changing decision, as the young baron will never again leave his home in the treetop. For all of evolutionary history, trees have provided both shelter and a habitat for countless living creatures, including the ancestors of today's humans, *Homo sapiens*. Many anthropologists believe that the process by which we became human did not begin until a few million years ago, when *Australopithecus* descended from the trees and evolved into *Homo erectus*. This key finding of evolution theory affects our self-perception as a species even today; hence our view of tree-dwellers, which some Indigenous peoples still are, as "primitive." Yet civilization need not be a one-way street, and it can even change direction, as Calvino's novel reminds us. It is only by choosing the supposedly "primitive" option that his baron is able to emancipate himself from the constraints of civilization.

The relationship between humans and trees is inseparable from the history of evolution, of civilization, and indeed of building. There are mythological, ecological, and economic strands of meaning woven into all of them. The frontispiece of the second edition (1755) of Marc-Antoine Laugier's *Essai sur l'architecture* of 1753 shows an allegory of Architecture reclining against the shattered remains of classical architecture (fragments of an Ionic column) and pointing to a "primitive hut" built out of trees and branches in a wild, untamed landscape (Fig 1). The image stands for the virtues of planning and building on the basis of the natural order. The trunks of living trees provide the primary structure, while as secondary elements, the walls and roof are made of branches and twigs. Laugier's programmatic demand that architecture return to "natural simplicity" was of a piece with the philosophical idea that society had departed from some pristine natural condition, as formulated by Rousseau at around the same time. Once humanity's origins, and hence architecture's origins, had been traced back to trees, those same trees inevitably became a focus of the yearning for a fresh start, even if both Rousseau and Laugier knew very well that the wheel of civilization cannot simply be thrown into reverse. It is nevertheless true that whenever our faith in progress falters, it tends to be nature that is invoked as the best wellspring of inspiration to draw on.

That was certainly the case in the early 1960s, when modernist architecture, having radically uncoupled itself from the limitations of history, location, and nature, increasingly came in for criticism. The groundbreaking exhibition, *Architecture Without Architects* curated by Bernard Rudofsky at New York's Museum of Modern Art in 1964, featured countless examples of vernacular building, including one that turned a living baobab tree into a human dwelling (Fig 2). Presenting this mighty, multi-generational tree as an alternative to a society that had completely sold out to technological progress was, of course, a deliberate provocation. The exhibition comprising 200 photographs of "non-pedigreed" buildings and structures, all of them the result of design and construction processes dictated by nature and the topographical and geological conditions prevailing in one particular location, inevitably cast doubt on the self-image of architecture then in the ascendancy. "No new way of building, a new way of living is needed," opined Rudofsky, even as early as 1937.

As a result of ever more complex planning processes and construction methods, the widespread use of computer-assisted design (CAD) and building information management (BIM), and, most recently, the encroachments of artificial intelligence (AI), the first two decades of the twenty-first century have seen architecture as a discipline become heavily dependent on technological progress. Yet, as is so often the case, this ever-greater reliance on technology has provoked critical counter-movements that want architecture to return to its natural origins. One such movement is *Baubotanik*, or botanical building, which was developed by Ferdinand Ludwig, a Munich-based architect and professor whose scientific experiments turn on the creation of new architectural structures built with living trees. Ludwig has studied both the history of building with living trees and the various ways in which this tradition is still practiced today, from the linden trees for dancing under in the villages of southern Germany to the treehouses of Polynesia and the living root bridges of northern India. The real radicalism of his concept, however, resides in his efforts to develop new methods for the future by drawing on the empirical findings of history. The discipline of *Baubotanik* that he himself founded explores the potential of living trees for the creation of new structures. It thus marks a clear departure from the creed of infinite acceleration based on the latest technological advances. Making nature the paramount consideration in all planning processes tends to have a decelerating effect; for although we humans have learned how to reprogram nature for our own purposes, the growth of trees is still tied to factors that are not so readily modified. Indeed, the fundamental truth at the heart of all the many options for using trees to create growing, living structures is this: *It will take time*. The idea of designing usable buildings with living trees may seem too utopian for some; after all, it runs counter to the notion of an ever-faster way of life driven by ever-faster technological progress. But when combined with scientific analysis and an experimental approach, it turns out to be less utopian than it perhaps appeared at first glance.

In recent years, the Architekturmuseum of the Technical University of Munich (TUM) has taken up the task of staging exhibitions to analyze and shed light on the directions that architecture may soon (have to) take, given the global challenges facing us. We began bridging the divide between architecture and its larger context of planned natural spaces with our 2017 exhibition *Out There: Landscape Architecture on Global Terrain*, in which five other chairs were involved. The exhibition *Trees, Time, Architecture!* is another interdisciplinary endeavor involving the TUM's adjacent chair of Green Technologies in Landscape Architecture and driven by our shared conviction that scientific inquiry into natural growth processes can deliver important insights for the future of building.

ANTHOLOGY OF MULTIPLE PERSPECTIVES ON A TREE
While this book mirrors the exhibition in part, it also extends it, deepening the themes that the exhibition could not fully express as it sought to orchestrate the narrative and balance its parts. But then it also does not extend it, in that the book embarks on a different road map to explore how the themes relate to each other. The exhibition is structured according to three broad but coherent sections: first, trees'

relation to dimensions and time; second, links between architecture and traditionally implemented trees; and finally, trees becoming living architecture—*Baubotanik*. This book, however, takes a more unpredictable approach: it sequences contributions, set in a magazine format, in no deliberate order and highlights the individuality of authors and their varied points of observation. Combining different genres— memoir, photo documentary, and scientific analysis, to mention a few— and the occurrence of the first-person perspective aim to help this book promote a tree as a cultural entity, as the lead character of various disciplines.

The tree appears as evidence of irrational political will in the film review of *Taming the Garden*, by filmmaker Salomé Jashi, who for over four years, tracked 200 "big and old" trees, purchased from the owners of their original homes, uprooted, and transported by all means through Georgia to settle in the garden of a politically mighty man. The tree becomes a medium for a biographical account in Mark Primack's memoir of how disciplinary histories escape being monolith and how, in parallel with the development of architecture's Modern Movement and its frictions, a genealogy of botanic architecture was taking place, too. The tree

Fig 2 Baobab tree, from Bernard Rudofsky, *Architecture Without Architects: An Introduction to Non-Pedigreed Architecture*, The Museum of Modern Art, New York, 1964, fig. 21

serves as both victim and perpetrator of a disaster in a regional economy in a striking photo documentary by Caimi Piccinni, who over seven years followed how the *Xylella fastidiosa*, a bacterial pathogen, has devastated olive groves in the Salento region of Italy, depicting chemical treatments, family stories, corruption, and human links with trees through grief, anger, and resilience. Trees' canopies become a place of escape, resistance, and rising feminism in Laura Leonelli's microhistory based on anonymous photography and cultural history, showing trees as fictive and real allies to women in their fight against the domination of patriarchy. Scientific portraits of trees were drawn by botanists in the eighteenth and nineteenth centuries following the development of forestry as a science and urban discipline, as narrated in Sonja Dümpelmann's essay following the accommodation of trees within civic spaces of streets and housing of the traditional Western city until eventually becoming a means of resistance, demanding the rights of trees in the US and Germany.

Further on, the tree becomes a drawing motif for landscape architects to develop in Noël van Dooren's drawing essay, which analyzes seven iconic landscape drawings in their attempts to show cyclical and linear time, growth history, and the relationship of trees with their surroundings. In Roberta Martufi's historical review, the tree is viewed from the perspective of the treehouse, observed as a precious and exclusive object over centuries, from the villas of Roman emperors to refuges of early Christian saints and dendrites, until becoming a public symbol of arcadian settlement among cypresses, cedars, lemons, and oranges in parks throughout Renaissance Europe. In the visionary and experimental designs of Édouard François and Office for Living Architecture, the tree is a sparring partner to affect the environment, build even large-scale, mainstream urban projects, and rethink principles of the construction industry. The beautiful and timeless *Ficus elastica* trees that form living root bridges in Khasi and Jaintia village communities in India carry the visual message of this exhibition and catalog most powerfully. Here, the tree appears *as found*; we cannot trace its beginnings, its history. It is a scene to remind, investigate, document, understand, and learn from. Numerous field trips of Ferdinand Ludwig, Kristina Pujkilović, and Wilfrid Middleton are reflected in the interview with Morningstar Khongthaw, a representative of communal activism for the preservation of this specific nature-culture, which escapes the Western understanding of landscape. Eventually, those learnings are channeled through a joint Indo-German educational project to test building practices and design methods for living architecture and systematized in a report following the interview (with Zijing Deng and Elahe Mahdavi also contributing). The tree as a keeper of Indigenous knowledge appears as well among the lines of the collaborative article by Kelly Church, Sam Jamero, Shelbi Nahwilet Meissner, Rico Newman, and Jana VanderGoot. An appealing sequence of short stories and visual shots, framed as making-as-research, follows a series of events and learning methods to jointly reproduce and mimic wooden Indigenous objects along the lines of cultural geography, land ethics, Indian tribes' tree stories, and a set of fabrication processes in which the hand, custom jigs, drill presses, and table saw equipment replace standardization by working with wood perceived as a spirit holder.

Without seeing the tree as a source of economic exploitation for construction, arguments raised in *Trees, Time, Architecture!* aim to explore only a cultural niche. The tree-as-a-product is *the* theme—explicitly and implicitly—contained in many aspects of the exhibition, from its contents and design to the outdoor installation *Baumlager*. On this, a particular statement comes from a conversation between the curators, and Michael Vollmer and Hannes Harter, which unfolds around conflicts among the lifespan of buildings and the growth rate of trees and the necessity for the rejection of the absolutist approaches when it comes to the predominance of one favored material for ecologically appropriate construction. These lines are permeated with stills from the film *One Hundred and Fifty Thousand Trees* by White Arkitekter, unpacking a timber project in Sweden and exploring the politics of "zero" through photographic triptychs of forest-factory-building, their supply chains, and their impacts on forests.

Multiple perspectives on trees in this book aim to leave open for the reader the possibility to envision their own proximity to either trees, time, or architecture. When Sigfried Giedion's *Space, Time and Architecture*, to which our title establishes a tentative analogy, was published in 1941, his idea was to write a dynamic "contemporary history" that is "a process, a pattern of living and changing attitudes and interpretations"[1] departing from the particular moment of the "march of industry"[2] in human surroundings. Inspired by Albert Einstein's theory of relativity proclaiming time and space as no longer absolute categories, Giedion opted for the marriage of art and science to create "dynamic equilibrium" with time as a fourth dimension for architects to restore harmony among man, machines, and nature. Opposed by Einstein, Giedion's book remained influential far more for its defense of Walter Gropius, the Bauhaus, and modernists than for offering hopeful scenarios for the organic integration of technology into social life. Some of Giedion's preoccupations still persist in the curatorial statement of *Trees, Time, Architecture!*, such as the shift from the design of finished objects towards the design of processes, an appeal for a mix of scientific and artistic approaches, and the reconciliation of the still contradictory relations of nature and culture.

Even the structure of this book, with its playful and vibrating visual arrangements, holds an analogy to Giedion's idea of the "picture book," "pictural way," or the collage novel, where text and images are partially detached from each other.[3] Nevertheless, more than eighty years later, belief in industrial progress is a long over, cohabitation extends from preoccupation with humanity and the universal man toward other species and genders; and science is needed beyond theoretical reflections but in its operative potential. Finally, "space" as a cosmic category of infinite expansion and the metaphysical preoccupation of modern architects is substituted with "trees," in an attempt to create both finite and local cohabitable realities based on alchemies of balance with all possible means, archives of the past and technologies of the future to support digital humanism. The exclamation mark may follow due to time.

ACKNOWLEDGMENT
Our sincere gratitude goes to Park Books editor Chris Reding for her generous advice and patience in working together on the contents of this book.

1—Sigfried Giedion, *Space, Time and Architecture: The Growth of a New Tradition* (Cambridge, MA: Harvard University Press, 1941), 5.
2—Giedion, *Space, Time and Architecture*, 244.
3—Filine Wagner, "Surrealist History: Mechanization Takes Command and Art as Method," in *Richard Hamilton-Sigfried Giedion. Reaper*, exhibition catalog (Geneva: JRP Ringer, 2017), 207; Arthur P. Molella, "Sigfried Giedion's Space, Time and Architecture and Mechanization Takes Command," in *Technology and Culture* 43, no. 2 (2002): 374–389.

Fig 1 Groupe Scolaire, Cornebarrieu. The 500 trees planted in and around Duncan Lewis' school are not just part of the landscape, but also an integral part of the architecture.

Ferdinand Ludwig, Kristina Pujkilović

TREES, TIME, ARCHITECTURE!

Trees have influenced life on Earth for a good 300 million years. They were the preferred habitat of our early ancestors, and their crowns count among the world's most biodiverse habitats even today. Trees supplied man's first building materials, and thousands of years later, primordial trees fossilized to coal fueled industrialization. Yet it is precisely because of that same intensive exploitation of our fossil resources over a relatively short period of time, and above all the carbon emissions resulting from it, that we now need trees more than ever before: both at the local level, to help us adapt to a changing climate, and at the global level, as a means of halting, and perhaps even reversing, climate change. As promising as trees are, however, the solutions they offer are neither simple nor instantly available; for not only do trees count among the largest, oldest, and most complex organisms on Earth, but they also grow extremely slowly. Their lifespans far outstrip any human lifetime, and the pace at which they grow is at odds with the ever-quickening pace of social, technological, and ecological change. At the same time, many of the trees we love and value most are not a product of wild, untamed nature, but rather the happy outcome of our own planting, pruning, cultivating, and hybridizing. It follows that our complex, and often contradictory, relationship with trees is bound to be a factor in any cultural history of humanity. We have deified them, feared them, built houses out of them, banished them from our cities, adorned high-rise buildings with them, and were clearing great tracts of forest long before the invention of the chainsaw.

ARBOREAL DIMENSIONS
Today's largest living tree is probably one of the coastal redwoods in Redwood National Park in California. It is approximately 115 meters tall and has an estimated volume of more than 500 cubic meters of wood. The oldest living tree is a nearly 5,000-year-old Great Basin bristlecone pine in California's White Mountains, though there are clonal tree colonies that are much older than that. The record in this category is

Fig 2 The Oerliker Park in Zurich (Studio Vulkan Landschaftsarchitektur) represents a process-based design strategy. Originally planned as a "tree hall" with 1,000 densely planted ash trees, today loosely arranged trees and a greater variety of species characterize the park's appearance.

Fig 3 The detail shows how structural steel elements grow into a living tree structure, forming a plant-technical composite construction.

held by Pando, a colony of quaking aspen in Utah, whose 40,000 trees on an area of more than 40 hectares are all offshoots of the same ancient root system, which, according to various model calculations, must be at least 14,000 years old.[1]

So there are living trees that are older than even the Pyramids of Gizeh as the most durable structures ever built by man. Even more astonishing is that at the time Pando put forth its first shoots, we humans were still hunter-gatherers and had yet to discover agriculture. Trees can grow to the height of a thirty-story building and can spread horizontally to the equivalent of some twenty Manhattan blocks. Furthermore, they accomplish these extraordinary feats by means of the same biochemical process that enables all plants to grow and thrive: photosynthesis. Using nothing more than sunlight as a source of energy, they convert water and carbon dioxide into sugar and oxygen and by doing so generate the building blocks of their own biomass. Any additional nutrients and trace elements needed are delivered by the water that trees take up from the soil. Photosynthesis, moreover, like all the other processes involved in creating the structure of a tree, takes place at a normal ambient temperature and pressure, making it utterly unlike the energy-intensive processes required to produce steel and concrete, as the standard building materials of today. Another point in trees' favor is that they actually bond carbon dioxide while at the same time emitting oxygen, whereas today's construction industry does the exact opposite, emitting vast quantities of the greenhouse gas carbon dioxide.

Such an outstanding track record is bound to impress us and might even tempt us to view trees as an all but inexhaustible source of renewable raw materials. Yet any realistic assessment of their potential has to take account the limitations of growth. To get a true sense of just how slowly trees grow, we need only visualize the volume of wood produced by a forest in a single year as a barely 1-millimeter-thick sheet of veneer covering the whole forest floor. Every year would see the addition of another such sheet until finally, in the mature forest, the forest floor would be covered by a wooden board of just a few centimeters thick. In the forest of Germany, to give an example, this board would be just 4 centimeters thick! And it need hardly be said that the quantities of timber used in architecture are invariably a multiple of that amount. To build a single-family dwelling out of solid wood, for example, you would need an area of forest equal to around twenty times the footprint of the house itself. And whereas such a house could be erected in a matter of days, it would take the forest around eighty years to produce the necessary volume of timber. Viewed in this light, buildings made of wood—that is, using trees as raw material—can be understood as compressing the forest in both time and space.

FOSSILIZED TREES
Trees served as firewood even before they were used for building. This was standard practice until industrialization, when coal took over as the primary source of energy. Coal has a significantly higher energy density than wood and was a key factor in rapid urban expansion, transport, and industry. The relationship between fossilized trees in the form of coal and living trees is therefore a special one. After all, it was coal that made possible the industrial production of "modern" building materials such as steel, and that, paradoxically, took the pressure off forests, which until then, in the pre-industrial age in particular, had been recklessly plundered as a source of building materials and fuel. Yet the burning of coal on a massive scale also had negative consequences, including the "acid rain" that in the late twentieth century killed off millions of trees. It was the dying forests of the uplands of Central Europe that in the 1980s drove tens of thousands of environmentalists out onto the streets and led to the election of the first members of the Green Party to the German parliament. Yet the predicted apocalypse and media-hyped doomsday scenarios failed to materialize. In fact, the danger posed by acid rain was averted remarkably fast both politically, through the passage of effective legislation, and technically, through the installation of filters. In retrospect, the "dying forests" of the late twentieth century do not look much like a crisis at all, and compared with the current situation seem little more than a footnote of history. Today, by contrast, fossil-fuel-driven economic growth on a global scale is causing greenhouse gas emissions to rise exponentially; and the climate crisis caused by the combustion of fossilized trees, among other factors, is destroying trees on an unprecedented scale, be it through forest fires or drought or their greater vulnerability to pests resulting from the same.

Many hope that biochar can put this process into reverse. If tree cuttings, for example, are anaerobically carbonized instead of being incinerated or composted, they retain much of their carbon content, which is thereby sequestered and permanently removed from the atmosphere. The end product is a high-quality raw material that can be used to upgrade poor soil. The underlying principle has been known for millennia, as is evidenced by the *terra preta de índio,* the fertile soils resulting from human intervention in the Amazon basin. But if the annual carbon emissions of an industrial powerhouse like Germany are compared with its annual output of biomass suitable for biochar production, it quickly becomes clear that only a fraction of the former can be offset by the latter. Or, to put it more bluntly, given the size of our forests and the stress they are already under as a consequence of climate change, it would be presumptuous to look to them for salvation. On the contrary, if we want to preserve our forests in the long run, we have to stop burning fossilized trees (and all other fossil fuels) right now.

URBAN TREES
The rapid global population growth, in conjunction with an equally rapid increase in urbanization, is turning urban areas into the focus of pressing ecological and social issues. Climate change, moreover, has long since ceased to be just a specter on the horizon and is already a reality that can be felt in our everyday lives—in overheated streets, for example. Trees can have a significant impact on temperatures in urban areas, both through the transpiration process and through the shade that they provide. They can counteract urban heat islands and enhance people's thermal well-being. Residents of neighborhoods with tree-lined streets are known to be signficantly less liable to cardiovascular and metabolic disease than are residents in the same age and income bracket of neighborhoods with fewer trees. Furthermore, the shade

and transpiration of trees planted close to a building help lower the amount of energy required to keep it cool. Nevertheless, decades or even centuries may have to pass before a tree reaches its full height and with it the maximum aesthetic and microclimatic impacts expected of it; and cities can change radically during that time. A tree planted in 1800 that is now at the height of its development, for example, will have experienced not only the rapid growth of cities that took place in the nineteenth century but also the destruction wrought by the Second World War, the reconstruction that followed it, and the late twentieth- and early twenty-first-century expansion of cities to include large residential suburbs and commercial zones. Fortunately, the late nineteenth century also saw the emergence of the Garden City movement as well as attempts to combine the best of both town and country by endowing the existing urban fabric with parks and leafy boulevards— an endeavor in which trees played a key role as the largest, and hence most impactful, elements for structuring whole neighborhoods. That cities should be green is now axiomatic, and trees have become a fixture of the cityscape for inhabitants of countless cities all over the world.

TREES IN ARCHITECTURE
Much less a matter of course than the use of trees in the urban space is their integration into buildings at the architectural level. Here, we can point to a number of historical examples and pioneering projects of recent years, but these buildings are by no means commonplace. Nevertheless, interest in the architectural use of living trees is rising sharply, in some cases building on the modern approaches of the twentieth century and in other cases revisiting the approaches of the premodern age. The arguments in favor of this appoach are almost always ecological, whether it is the impact of trees on microclimate described above, the improved air quality, or the promotion of biodiversity. In principle, there can be no objections to such arguments, especially at a time when we are facing a range of ecological crises. But anyone who takes a critical look behind the leafy canopy will soon realize how enormously expensive it is to plant large-crowned trees on high-rises, for example. Nor are the costs exclusively financial. The ecological downsides may even outweigh the benefits, as when a structure has to be reinforced, which is bound to translate into extra building materials and hence higher emissions. In some cases such trees placed on highrise buildings are really no more than "fig leaves" for the greenwashing of conventional architecture. Having said that, it would not be fair to single out today's construction industry for punishment, notwithstanding its voracious appetite for raw materials and energy. We should instead be trying to understand the historical context on which contemporary architecture with trees draws for inspiration. Two distinct lines of development can be made out here. The first of these is the tradition of functional green architecture that incorporates trees to perform specific tasks. The regularly trimmed hedges planted to protect the windward walls of old farmhouses and outbuildings are a good example of this. As a practice born of necessity, such hedges are very different from the trees included in architectural ensembles primarily for reasons of pleasure and prestige. The legendary Hanging Gardens of Babylon might be viewed almost as a prototype of such creations, being at once inordinately extravagant and an almost superhuman feat of horticultural engineering. Before rushing to use trees for ecologically and socially equitable architecture, therefore, we would do well to pay attention to which tradition we are drawing on and to consider the direct and indirect consequences that our actions may have.

TREES AS ARCHITECTURE
Trees, time, and architecture are in a very special relationship when trees are not only placed opposite architecture, but become an integral part of a structure or a structure is formed entirely from living trees. This is the approach of *Baubotanik*, which although in its infancy as a design discipline, as a practice can look back on a tradition as long as it is fascinating. The most impressive historical examples include the living root bridges of the Khasi People, which as green infrastructure are to be found in large numbers throughout the subtropical mountain forests of Meghalaya Province in northeastern India. It takes several generations to build such a living bridge, meaning that children build on the preparatory work done by their parents, knowing that only their own children—or even grandchildren—will actually get to use the structure. These days,

such long-term thinking and acting has become all but unknown in the Western world, despite being more urgently needed than ever before. And time is running out. It is therefore vital that a contemporary approach to *Baubotanik* is seaking for compromises. As important as it is to develop design methods that respect the slow growth of trees, we must also acknowledge the advantages of using technical solutions to create large green structures fast.

EXHIBITION
The exhibition *Trees, Time, Architecture!—Design in Constant Transformation* aims to visualize and shed light on the fascinating, fraught, and often paradoxical relationship between these three factors. Only then can we identify those possibilities, and seize those opportunities, that will enable us to build a livable future both for ourselves and for the greater part of the Earth's flora and fauna. The design disciplines of architecture and landscape architecture have a key role to play here—at least if we can extrapolate the lessons to be learned from them and apply them on a global scale, sounding out new alliances with artistic and scientific approaches en route. Drawing on historical and topical examples from very different cultural contexts and climatic zones, the exhibition examines the potential of "building on trees" for both architecture and landscape architecture—as well as the contradictions it brings with it. It also sheds light on the tensions that inevitably exist between the slowness of tree growth and the urgency of the task at hand, which is to find solutions to a whole raft of social and ecological problems. But the total lifespan of trees must be taken into account and viewed in relation to the temporary nature of functional requirements as well as sociocultural, technological, architectural, and urbanist developments. This is the first time that an exhibition project has homed in on the thematic complex of trees, time, and architecture and viewed it from a multidimensional perspective. What it reveals is the need for a paradigm shift away from the design of finished objects and towards the design of processes with which to establish a fruitful and sustainable relationship between trees and buildings.

This catalog is an invitation to engage more deeply with the issues raised by the exhibition. It is supplemented by a digital index of all the projects presented in the exhibition that is permanently available here:[2]

1–For further details and references to the examples and figures mentioned in this text, please go to the book Ferdinand Ludwig and Daniel Schönle, *Growing Architecture—How to Design and Build with Trees*, (Basel: Birkhäuser Verlag, 2023).
2–https://www.arc.ed.tum.de/en/gtla/trees-time-architecture/

Fig 4   The protective hedges in the area around Monschau, Germany, were planted and regularly trimmed to protect farmhouses and courtyards in windy areas.

...o biloba and *Betula alba* along Semperstraße in Dresden, c. 1930. From Victor Buchholz, "...ächerbaum' Ginkgo biloba L. als Straßenbaum," *Gartenflora* 81, no. 10 (1932): 243.

Sonja Dümpelmann

TREE FUTURES
How Past Ideas Can Foster a Plant-Friendly Urban Future

Trees elicit human affection and attention. One reason for this is that they connect us to the past and the future, emotionally and economically. Once seeded or planted, trees describe a moment in the past, yet they live in the present, and they will grow in the future. Human cultures have developed under and alongside trees. Humans have worshipped them and used them as materials, markers, memorials, and metaphors. In Nordic myth, the ash tree Yggdrasil stands at the center of the world as a cosmological symbol. Its roots reach into the underworld while its branches embrace the heavens, thus connecting past and future as well as sky, earth, and everything below. Hindus and Buddhists attribute a similar cosmological meaning to the sacred fig tree, which, in contrast to the Yggdrasil, is often represented as rooting in the heavens and sending its branches with creative energies down to earth.

Tree time, that means, trees' perpetual state of becoming, is essential for human well-being, and humans have worked with trees throughout their history. The woody plants have been a renewable resource of energy and timber, and they provide what today are often referred to as ecosystem services. By intercepting stormwater, protecting against erosion, providing shade and evapotranspiration, sequestering carbon, and producing oxygen, trees enhance the health and comfort of our human living environments; in fact, together with all other plants they are essential for human survival on Earth. Nevertheless, or perhaps rather because of this, trees and the landscapes they form, have also been contested. Consider, for example, trees standing in the way of new construction. Trees that, through common forest rights including pannage and foraging for food and fuel, provided livelihoods for many, have been removed to provide livelihoods for a few. Trees were felled to build human settlements, and then reinserted into urban areas years, decades, or centuries later.

Given trees' importance for human life and their relative permanence, they have inspired pragmatic foresight as well as conservative impulses. This has been the case despite many humans' difficulty to think beyond two generations. The idea of planting and saving trees for posterity is revealed in fifteenth-century treatises and court cases of several European states.[1] In the German states in the eighteenth century, cameralists, silviculturists, arboriculturists, and landscape gardeners began to think more systematically about planting trees for a time that reached well beyond the lives of their children. This foresight was founded on a belief in divine creation and progress, driven by economic interests and a search for enduring prosperity and happiness among the ruling classes. Foresters' futures thinking involving the fourth dimension and the eighteenth-century idea of sustainable yield soon spread beyond the German states and Europe. It became part of colonial practices that have been complicit in exploiting and extracting labor and resources, in enforcing or covering-up social disparities and harm, and in serving racist political objectives. It is a paradox of history that the concept of sustainable yield ultimately led to the creation of socially and environmentally unsustainable forests; that it was developed to produce the timber for extractive industries of finite resources such as silver and iron ores; and that the pollution produced by these same industries further harmed the trees.

Nevertheless, the idea of sustainability, and especially its implications of time and foresight as practiced (or not) in past centuries, has relevance for today's environmental stewardship, including urban and landscape design. Arguably, foresight can be employed to shape future ways of living that are more truly sustainable socially, culturally, environmentally, and economically.

PYRAMIDS
The idea of time as the fourth dimension in silviculture became prominent in many German publications that established the field of forestry science (*Forstwissenschaft*) in the second half of the eighteenth

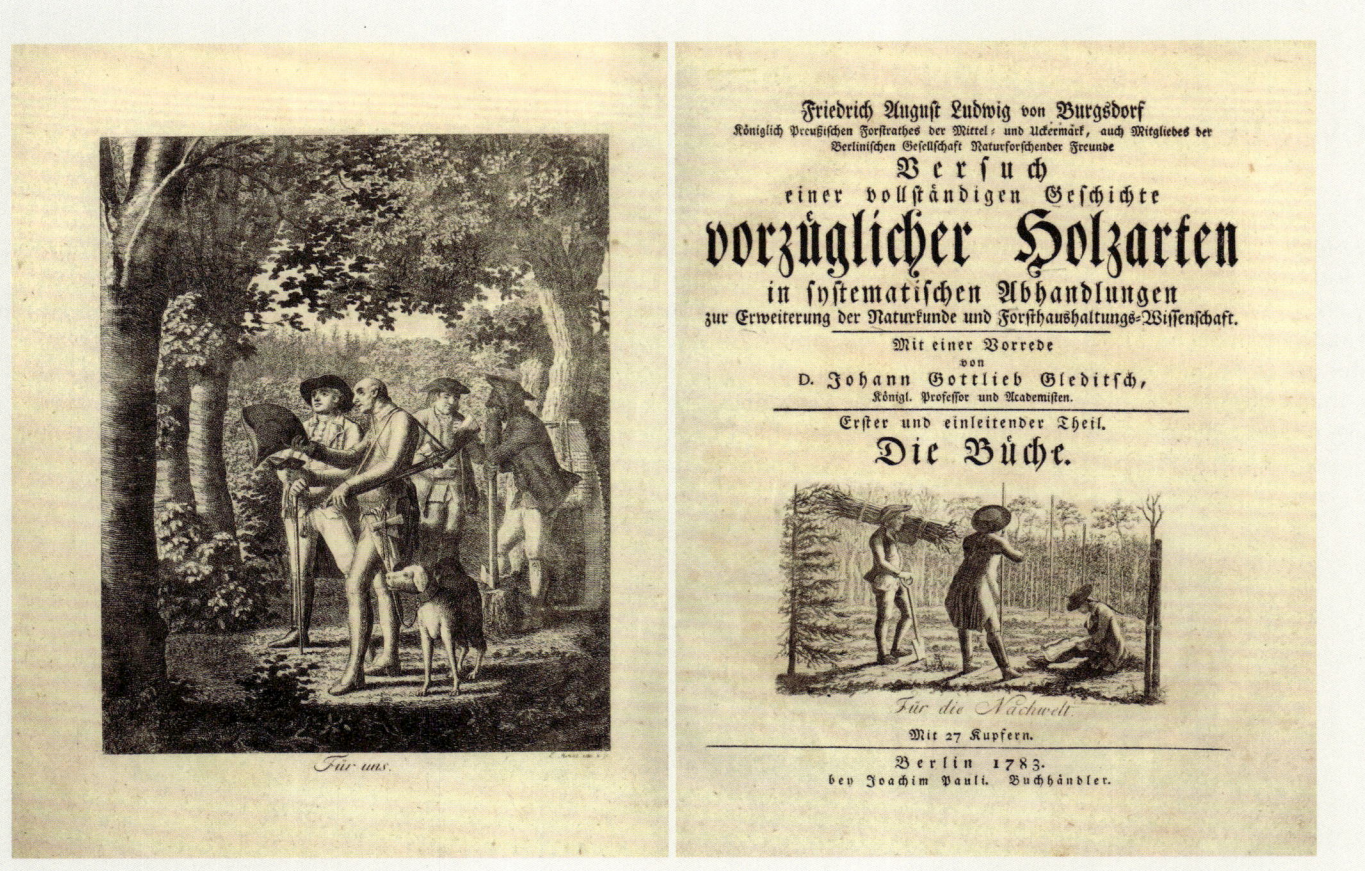

Fig 2   Frontispiece and title page from Friedrich August Ludwig von Burgsdorf, *Versuch einer vollständigen Geschichte vorzüglicher Holzarten, Erster und einleitender Teil: Die Buche* (Berlin: Joachim Pauli, 1783)

century after Hans Carl von Carlowitz explicitly established sustainable yield as a forestry principle in his *Sylvicultura Oeconomica* as early as 1713. Von Carlowitz described how demand and supply of timber should be kept in balance to secure the needs of future generations.[2] For the purposes of sustainable forestry German foresters turned trees and the forests they formed into abstract numbers and mathematical formulas.[3] Tables were drawn up to facilitate forecasting the yield for periods of up to two hundred years. In 1819, Georg Ludwig Hartig, one of the foundational forest scientists, exemplified the practice by printing a table that plotted out time until the year 2019.[4] Accounting for the time it took trees to grow was a challenge for foresters, as Hartig's colleague Heinrich Cotta, director of Saxony's royal forest academy, noted in the 1820s.[5] Yet, it was part of educated foresters' bread and butter. Good foresters, Cotta argued, kept a balance between harvest and planting to prevent soil depletion. After all, "forests grew best where humans—and consequently forestry science—were absent."[6] But human activity had caused wood scarcity in the first place, he noted, which forestry science was now to counteract.[7]

Lest the process of quantifying wood and explaining the science would lead to losing sight of the woods for the trees, illustrations in some of the early treatises reminded readers of the overall sustainability principle. Copperplates illustrating the concept framed Friedrich August Ludwig von Burgsdorf's first volume of his *Versuch einer vollständigen Geschichte vorzüglicher Holzarten* (Attempt at a comprehensive history of preferential woody species) (Fig 2). The frontispiece shows an estate owner carrying a gun over his shoulder, accompanied by his hunting dog and framed by mature trees. Gesticulating into the distance, he appears to be giving directions to the forester standing next to him with an open notebook. Two laborers stand behind the men, ready to carry out instructions and fell trees. The frontispiece is captioned "Für uns" (for us). It is to be read together with the smaller image on the opposite title page, showing several laborers using various tools and a plan to prepare for the planting of saplings. This image is fittingly captioned "Für die Nachwelt" (for posterity).[8]

Less kinetic, and more static, yet expressing the same message, was the motif of an etching printed barely a decade later, in 1792, on the title page of *Über nordamerikanische Bäume und Sträucher als Gegenstände der deutschen Forstwirtschaft und schönen Gartenkunst* (On North American trees and shrubs as objects in German forestry and garden art), written by physician and botanist Friedrich Casimir Medicus (Fig 3).[9] A stone pyramid stands at the center of a circular emblem. The words "Der Nachwelt heilig" (holy to posterity) and "Forst-Wirthschaft" (forest economy) spell out its symbolism. Like pyramids, which represented the afterlife and infinity, thus creating a connecting link between the earth and the heavens, and standing for strength, stability, and great societal accomplishments, sustainable forestry formed a strong foundation for future societal wealth. As an architectural monument with deep-seated cultural connotations often associated with divine providence (and appropriated variously for purposes ranging from tomb stones to ice cellars), the pyramid appeared to contemporary foresters as a fitting symbol and simile to legitimize their practice.

The emblematic use of the pyramid for understanding tree life also played an important role over half a century later. Then it was a specific pyramid, that of the Egyptian king Cheops and one of the seven wonders of the ancient world, which featured in an extraordinary chart drawn up by former Holstein forestry official Eduard Mielck to measure the tallest plants against architectural monuments, entitled *Die Riesen der Pflanzenwelt und die Riesengebilde der Baukunst* (The giants of the plant world and the giant structures of the art of building) (Fig 4).[10] Mielck had learnt his occupation at the Kiel forestry school (Kieler Forstlehranstalt) and worked as forester on private estates and in public office before he became a public road conductor and drafted a building ordinance for the Prussian province of Schleswig-Holstein. The chart combined Mielck's passion for trees with his occupational interests in construction and infrastructure. The drawing was part of a book on notable large and old trees around the world, published in 1863. Witnessing the increasing encroachments upon the world's arboreal heritage, Mielck warned of the ensuing loss of natural and cultural heritage and of the sense of history. His generation had inherited large trees from its forebears but whether and for how long these would be left for posterity was unclear. Inspired by the scarcity of information on tree age, Mielck collected data, catalogued the "dendrological

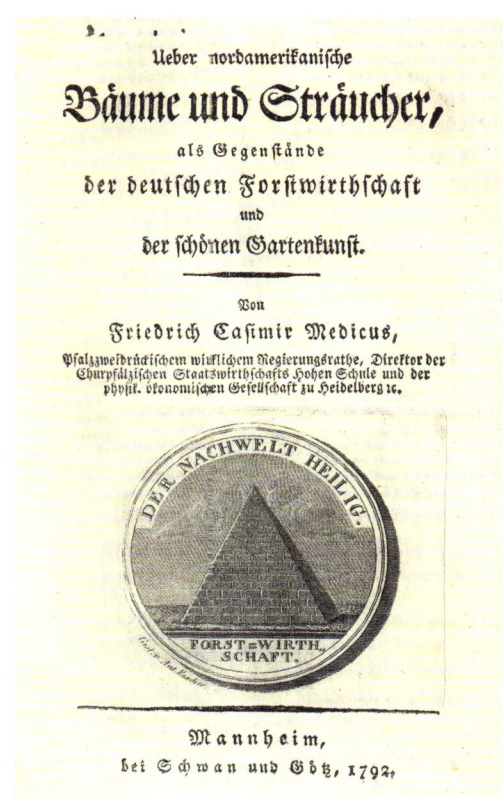

Fig 3   Title page from Friedrich Casimir Medicus, *Ueber nordamerikanische Bäume und Sträucher als Gegenstände der deutschen Forstwirthschaft und der schönen Gartenkunst* (Mannheim: Schwan und Götz, 1792)

Fig 4   Eduard Mielck's chart juxtaposing notable trees and architectural monuments, entitled *Die Riesen der Pflanzenwelt und die Riesengebilde der Baukunst* (The giants of the plant world and the giant structures of the art of building). Eduard Mielck, *Die Riesen der Pflanzenwelt* (Leipzig: Winter'sche Verlagsbuchhandlung, 1863), plate xvi

biometrics" of numerous trees, and drew portraits of select individuals as well as the comparative chart. The chart juxtaposes the Cheops pyramid with a giant sequoia, and the famous Tenerife dragon tree described by Alexander von Humboldt with the obelisk standing on Rome's Piazza di San Giovanni in Laterano. Among the foregrounded woody plants in this drawing are an "ancient German oak tree," a eucalyptus tree, a Norfolk pine, a Douglas fir, a common fir, a wax palm, the famous Sydney fig tree (known as the Port Jackson fig), and the still-existing chestnut tree, known as Castagno dei cento Cavalli, growing near Mount Etna. The trees are set against a backdrop created by the outlines of the largest contemporary architectural monuments. These include the cupolas of St. Peter's in Rome and St. Paul's in London, the steeples of Europe's major cathedrals, the Torre degli Asinelli in Bologna, the Luxor Obelisk in Paris, and to draw a local relationship, Hamburg's water tower (in the central district of Rothenburgsort). To add human and animal proportions, Mielck complemented his chart with a human figure, an elephant, and a whale in a tank.[11] However, as important as the comparison of horizontal, circumferential, and especially vertical dimensions is Mielck's collection of tree lifespans—that is, the fourth dimension. It ranges from what at the time was thought to be 300 years for north German pine trees to 5,150 years for Senegalese baobabs. These had been ranked already in the previous century as among the oldest living plants known on Earth at the time.[12]

Questions regarding tree age and death were topics of increasing interest in the first half of the nineteenth century.[13] French botanist Achille Richard dedicated some pages to data on tree age and size in his 1822 overview of plant life, and in 1831 his famed colleague Augustin Pyramus de Candolle wrote an entire treatise on the topic, urging the collection of tree age data and, similar to Mielck some decades later, promoting the protection of old trees as natural monuments.[14] On the British continent in the 1840s, physician Alexander Harvey shared his "observations on the nature, longevity, and size of trees" with members of the Philosophical Society of Aberdeen.[15]

Do trees die of old age, or can they live forever if not harmed by externalities? Researchers are still pursuing these questions today, and they disagree.[16] But then as now there has also been consensus. We know that many slow-growing species can survive several thousand years and that trees mostly die of other causes than age.[17]

PATTERNS

The text and images in Mielck's book are infused with a romantic deference to old trees. Only a few decades later, towards the end of the nineteenth century, romanticism and an increasing nationalist sentiment became perceptible in new suggestions for forestry practice. By this time, the forests planted following instructions by von Burgsdorf and others had revealed their weaknesses. In the name of sustainability, von Burgsdorf and his colleagues had standardized seeding and planting practices, suggesting, for example, that a phalanx of male and female day laborers move across terrain digging plant holes, followed by an offset row of half the number of children sowing seeds in the respective holes to their right and left.[18] The outcome was monotonous tree patterns that lacked wildlife and interest, depleted the soil, and were increasingly susceptible to storms, fires, insects, and other potentially harmful impacts.

The Silesian squire, forester, and conservative politician Heinrich von Salisch reacted by formalizing the concept of forest aesthetics in an 1885 book with the homonymous title (*Forstästhetik*). Forest aesthetics was not an entirely new idea. Von Salisch's older colleagues, Bavarian forester W.F. Freiherr von der Borch and Saxon forester Gottlob König had already sketched out the general contours from the 1820s in essays on "the aesthetics in the forest" („Die Ästhetik im Walde") and "the poetry of silviculture" („Die Poesie des Waldbaues").[19] But some forty years later, von Salisch aspired to establish forest aesthetics as a practical subfield of both forestry and landscape gardening. This new field aimed at turning the forest into a total work of art that was publicly accessible and struck a balance between utility and beauty. This useful and aesthetically pleasing forest offered visual, olfactory, and auditory experiences. Forest aesthetics was to encourage forest and wildlife conservation and to forge collective identity and nationalist sentiment. However, this was to be achieved by curtailing foraging and other traditional common-use rights, which von Salisch considered to be disturbing to the forests' calm unless they were formalized and transferred to those already working in the forest or out of work only temporarily.[20]

Regardless of whether producing a rationalized monoculture or romanticized and naturalized forest scenes, forest management overall remained an exclusionary practice. By the time *Forstästhetik*'s third edition was published in 1911, foresters and landscape designers had taken note, and its ideas fed into the nature protection efforts of the Heimatschutz movement, ultimately serving nationalist-*völkisch* ideologies.[21]

Rather than monocultures and clear-cuttings, large old trees, lush undergrowth, and species diversity characterized the forests that von Salisch promoted and planted. Foresight and sustainable yield were now put to use in support of more variable planting patterns. Forest margins and driveways could be lined with different species, and they could alternate along allées and country roads, von Salisch suggested. Aesthetics and economics played a role in these choices, as did climatological aspects, especially trees' shade and drainage functions. For example, the long-standing tradition of planting fruit trees along country roads was a logical choice as it offered both seasonal color and annual fruit harvests. But timber trees could also be made to fit the bill. Slow-growing and late-leafing oaks alternating with fast-growing, early-leafing birches or mountain ash trees could provide interest throughout the seasons and serve as perpetual timber supply without risking the loss of an allée's general form and character.

What von Salisch visualized in diagrammatic plans (Fig 5), his French colleague, the arboriculturist Adolphe Chargueraud illustrated in sectional drawings (Fig 6). Chargueraud proposed what he called a perpetual planting pattern, the *plantation perpétuelle,* which he exemplified by drawing up a 120-year tree-planting plan for country roads. In this plan, which was based on 30-year harvest cycles, four species created different patterns over a period extending from 1870 until 1990. The first planting consisted of one ash tree alternating with two Lombardy poplars. Thirty years later, the poplars would be felled. In the place of two poplars one elm would be planted. Another thirty years on, and the original sixty-year-old ash trees would be taken down, to be replaced by columnar poplars. The latter would be felled after thirty years and replaced by elms. After another thirty-year interval, the older elms, now ninety years old, would be felled, and each one of them replaced by two Lombardy poplars. Chargueraud's *plantation perpétuelle* of fast- and slow-growing tree species would provide continuous shade and timber yield along the road.[22]

The movement away from monocultures towards the diversification of tree species, be it inside forests or outside along country roads and urban streets, was motivated by various experiences of loss and disaster, building upon the realization that extensive plantations of one species increased their vulnerability and often lacked aesthetic interest. In the early twentieth century, Dutch elm disease inspired the diversification of urban tree canopies in various ways. After affecting the trees in Dresden in the 1920s, ginkgo trees were hailed as a new addition to the desirable species list. The interplanting of ginkgos and white birches (*Betula alba*), as carried out as early as

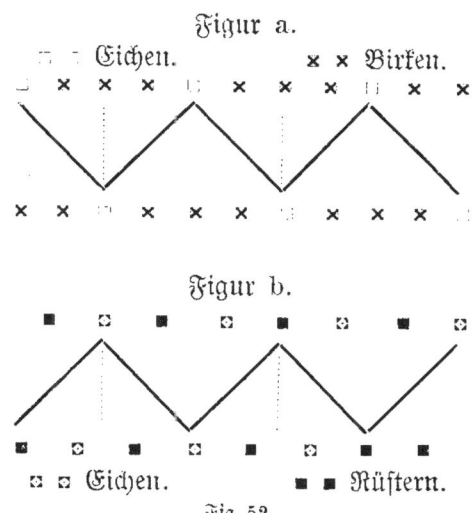

Fig 5 Diagrams illustrating planting patterns with alternating tree species for allées. The trees connected by lines would be left standing longterm. Von Salisch favored model (a) in which the interplanted fast-growing species (e.g. birches) would ultimately be felled, leaving regular, albeit offset, rows of the slow-growing species (e.g., oaks). Model (b), with offset rows of trees on either side of the road, would require maintaining species diversity and taking out two neighboring trees to maintain a regular rhythm. From Heinrich von Salisch, *Forstästhetik* (Berlin: Julius Springer, 1885), 192.

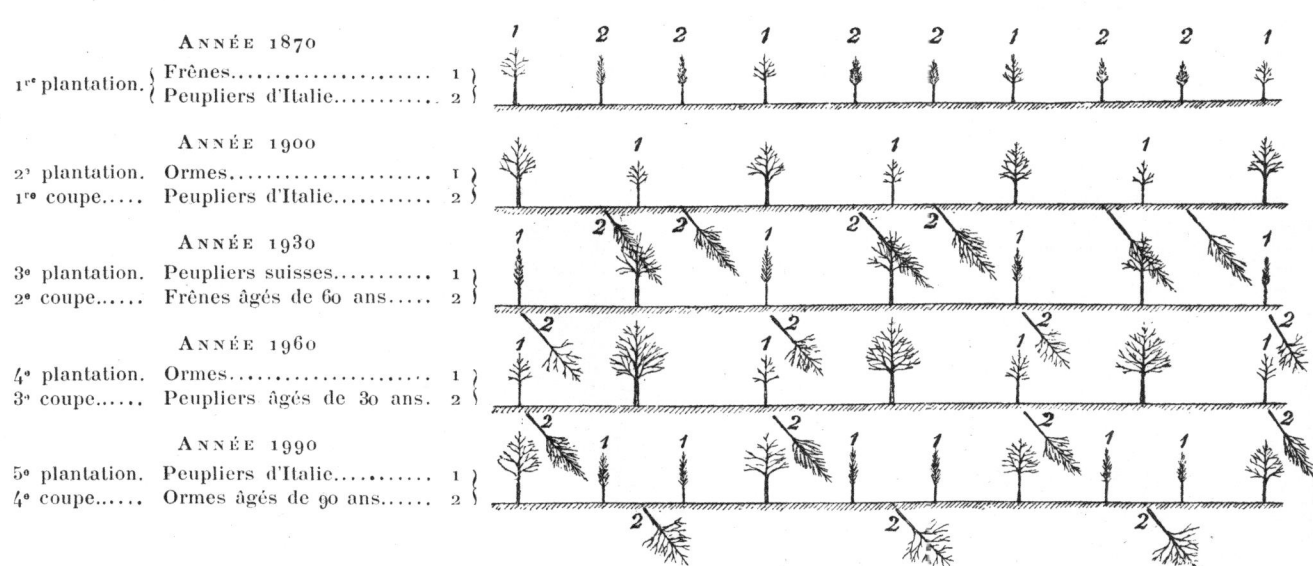

Fig 6 The *plantation perpétuelle*. From A. Chargueraud, *Les arbres de la ville de Paris. Traité des Plantations dans les villes et sur les routes départementales* (Paris: J. Rothschild, 1896), fig. 221.

1890 along the city's Semperstraße, was considered satisfying from all points of view, not least the aesthetic one (Fig 1).[23] Harmony was thought to be achieved through the contrast of the ginkgos' pyramidal crowns and their grey trunks with the birches' feathery, slightly drooping canopies above white stems. Along Hamburg's streets, the interplanting of oaks and mountain ash were considered successful. Ultimately, only the slow-growing oaks would be left standing, while the faster-growing mountain ash were felled.[24] Nevertheless, inter-planting along city streets did not become the norm.

In the United States in the mid-twentieth century, Dutch elm disease caused Chicago's residents and urban officials to learn the hard way. The disease caused the death of American elm trees, the dominant species lining the city's streets. The contingent coincidence of this and other local, national, and global circumstances in the late 1960s and early 1970s, led Chicago's urban foresters and city officials to reenvision the city as a sustainable, comprehensively managed urban forest that not only offered shade and beauty, but also provided a renewable timber resource.[25] On the local level there was a sudden emergence of large quantities of diseased and dead wood that needed to be disposed of. The recently passed municipal and state laws for environmental protection that prohibited the open burning of the wood debris further aggravated the problem. On the national level, domestic energy politics caused a lack of spare production capacity and a shortage of refinery capacity, while the 1967 Air Quality Act fueled oil consumption. As a consequence, on the global scale, the country's dependence on oil imports increased, a situation that was exacerbated by particularly cold winters in the early 1970s and complicated by the 1973 oil embargo by the Arab oil producing countries. The embargo contributed to a heightened environmentalism, and it induced national, state, and local leaders to call for measures to conserve energy and draw attention to alternative, renewable energy sources, including wood.

In this situation the young urban forester Charles A. Stewart developed ideas for recycling wood and using its revenue for the new planting and care of the decimated urban forest. It appeared best to use the wood as a renewable energy source by firing it in a newly built waste incinerator. In this way, the problem was no longer one of the "disposal of a nuisance," but rather one of recycling or the "recovery of a resource," as Stewart explained in 1974.[26] He also argued that timber production could be integrated into the management of urban forests from the beginning. The aim would be to establish a sustainable-yield system in which the revenues earned from tree harvesting would pay for the removal and replacement of dead trees. Scientific forestry applied to urban forestry meant that optimum stocking levels needed to be determined, rotations established, and the timber harvested at an optimum time, i.e., before the trees' maintenance costs rose. To reduce overall maintenance costs the choice of site-specific species would be preferable. Stewart suggested mixing three or four fast-growing species with quality hardwood species. In this way sizeable trees could be retained along streets and in front of homes, while others were harvested when their maintenance costs were still low and when they provided the best market-value timber. Mixing species also produced visual interest and safeguarded against the effects of epidemics like Dutch elm disease.

To turn Chicago into a productive, sustainable, and self-sustaining forest, Stewart overlaid the rectangular city map with a grid of management units covering approximately 65 hectares each. Arborists were to carry out their work by sectors, rotating through the entire city. The work in one sector had to be finished before labor in the next one began. In this way regular pruning (except for special needs and requests) would occur in each sector every five to seven years. To encourage age and species variety, prevent clearcutting, and reduce the trees' vulnerability to disease, Stewart suggested planting species with different optimal harvest cycles next to one another. This idea was not dissimilar to Chargueraud's *plantations perpétuelles*. Besides their climatological and aesthetic functions, trees in Chicago's urban forest were now also attributed with economic value in a very material sense, as timber for producing renewable energy. Chicago's project was never realized as envisioned. But by conceiving of the entire urban area as a forest, the plans expanded upon the foresighted planting in previous centuries when trees on medieval European fortifications supplied timber during sieges, and when former hunting parks were turned into forest commons and then into recreational public parks.

PROVISIONS

The Chicago story reveals the relevance of foresighted tree planting and care in urban areas. In cities especially, trees occupy contested space. How old they can grow in urban contexts is dependent not only on the site conditions and space but also on whether and how they are taken care of. Tree care takes time; time, that is often expended unevenly across urban terrain. Then as now, it is often poor neighborhoods that lack trees. Aside from structural discrimination including public disinvestment, residents in these neighborhoods suffer from the lack of time. Residents working multiple jobs to make ends meet have little time (and financial resources) to care for their own families, let alone for trees. Consequently, in countries like the United States where urban trees often do not receive sufficient attention from urban governments, "tree deserts" have developed in marginalized communities, with higher summer temperatures and higher levels of air pollution than in leafy neighborhoods and suburbs. Since the second half of the nineteenth century, "leafy" has not only been used to describe vegetated and tree-lined built environments; it also implies affluence thus equating trees with wealth.[27] Scholars have shown that funding programs that prioritize tree planting over tree care reproduce disinvestment and perpetuate racialized uneven development.[28]

It is no wonder then that in the nineteenth- and twentieth-century United States, tree planting and care partly relied on an economy of time that merged middle- and upper-class female volunteer work with philanthropy. The American women who lobbied for

Fig 7 Cartoon used by the Newark Shade Tree Commission to lobby citizens' support in tree care. From "Educating the People to Care for the Trees," *Park and Cemetery and Landscape Gardening* 22, no. 12 (1913): 302.

forest and urban tree planting were mostly privileged and White, yet largely deprived of educational and professional opportunities.[29] The organization of planting campaigns was an opportunity to enlarge their realm of influence and transgress the private and public spheres by extending their domestic care work to urban and other environments.

Whereas tree planting has been a common act of statesmen and -women of all political convictions to mark and memorialize important events, initiatives, and locations, it has also been central in environmental and human rights movements. Tree time, i.e., trees' multigenerational lifespans and purported permanence, have been important in this regard; as have been trees' physical character traits benefiting human health, and their use as synecdoche for nonhuman nature at large. During the American Civil Rights protests in the 1960s, tree planting and care became grassroots activities undertaken by Black residents in rundown New York City neighborhoods. With the help of trees, they asserted their rights to the city and made public space more livable.[30] In the 1980s in East Berlin, citizens used tree plantings to create alternative public spheres and ultimately counter publics that opposed the state and its environmental politics. Tree planting became part and parcel of the opposition movement against the German Democratic Republic's dictatorship that ultimately contributed to its fall in November 1989.[31]

Although often not as visible, the foresight and care integral to these activist tree plantings were a means of resistance and a way for citizens to (re)claim their right to the city. While arguments for the human right *to* trees were central in many urban tree planting activities in the nineteenth and twentieth centuries (even if not always realized), the rights *of* trees were also beginning to be recognized. In the early twentieth century, they were not yet based upon the elaborate arguments and theories put forward by today's legal scholars, but early traces can be found, for example, in a cartoon for a twentieth-century urban tree campaign by Newark's Shade Tree Commission in the United States (Fig 7). To garner volunteer citizen support, the commission anthropomorphized trees marching in file and holding placards demanding "Give us more water!," "Loosen the ground around us!," and "we're choking." Notably, some placards implicitly emphasize collaboration and cohabitation when they asked for "Reciprocity, shade for water," and demanded equivocally "Give us a legal opening." Furthermore, on Arbor Day in 1915, Newark's trees petitioned citizens to protect and care for them in an elaborately designed document printed on cardboard and signed by "Col. Kentucky Coffee," "Big Brave White Oak," "Miss Cellaneous," and others "on behalf of all Trees of city and forest." Decades before legal scholar Christopher D. Stone's pathbreaking article "Should Trees Have Standing?," which argued in 1972 that "forests, oceans, rivers and other so-called 'natural objects' in the environment" should have legal rights that could be asserted by recognized guardians, trees were made to assert their standing. The cartoon and pamphlet set an early example of using the mutual relationship between trees and humans to promote an environmental ethics that was based upon the idea of future communal life on one planet.[32]

The ideas of foresight and time entangled in past Western silvi- and arboriculture can be worth reconsidering in today's processes of transformation. The lessons learnt and opportunities missed presented here, albeit briefly, stand alongside the rich, manifold ideas of foresight and time vis-à-vis the more-than-human world imagined and practiced by members of Indigenous cultures around the world. Together, they can form a basis for aspiring towards tree futures that shape (urban) forests that are more socially just, environmentally sensitive, and culturally and economically sustainable.

1–Paul Warde, *The Invention of Sustainability: Nature and Destiny, c. 1500–1870* (Cambridge, UK: Cambridge University Press, 2018), 58–91.

2–Hans Carl von Carlowitz, *Sylvicultura oeconomica* (Leipzig: Braun, 1713), 98, 105. For von Carlowitz and the idea of sustainability, also see Ulrich Grober, *Die Entdeckung der Nachhaltigkeit—Kulturgeschichte eines Begriffs* (Munich: Antje Kunstmann Verlag, 2013), English translation by Ray Cunningham: *Sustainability— A Cultural History* (Totnes, UK: Green Books, 2012).

3–Henry E. Lowood, "The Calculating Forester: Quantification, Cameral Science, and the Emergence of Scientific Forestry Management in Germany," in *The Quantifying Spirit in the Eighteenth Century*, eds. Tore Frängsmyr, J.L. Heilbron, and Robin E. Rider (Berkeley: University of California Press, 1990), 315–342.

4–Georg Ludwig Hartig, *Neue Instructionen für die königlich-preußischen Geometer und Forst-Taxatoren* (Berlin: Kummerische Buchhandlung zu Leipzig, 1819).

5–Heinrich Cotta, *Anweisung zum Waldbau, 4te verbesserte Auflage* (Dresden and Leipzig: Arnoldsche Buchhandlung, 1828), vii.

6–"Die Wälder bilden sich und bestehen also da am besten, wo es gar keine Menschen–und folglich auch gar keine Forstwissenschaft giebt;" Cotta, *Anweisung zum Waldbau*, iii.

7–Cotta, *Anweisung zum Waldbau*, iv.

8–Friedrich August Ludwig von Burgsdorf, *Versuch einer vollständigen Geschichte vorzüglicher Holzarten, Erster und einleitender Teil: Die Buche* (Berlin: Joachim Pauli, 1783).

9–Friedrich Casimir Medicus, *Ueber nordamerikanische Bäume und Sträucher als Gegenstände der deutschen Forstwirthschaft und der schönen Gartenkunst* (Mannheim: Schwan und Götz, 1792).

10–For Mielck and his chart, also see Sonja Dümpelmann, "Plants," in *The Landscape Project*, eds. Richard Weller and Tatum Hands (Los Angeles: ORO, 2022), 52–68.

11–A similar size comparison and juxtaposition of architectural monuments (Cheops pyramid, Freiburg cathedral, and Brandenburg Gate) with a giant sequoia can be found in the 1978 book *Tree Ecology and Preservation* (Amsterdam, Oxford, New York: Elsevier Scientific Publishing Company) by A. Bernatzky.

12–Eduard Mielck, *Die Riesen der Pflanzenwelt* (Leipzig: Winter'sche Verlagsbuchhandlung, 1863), figure xvi, 121–24. For an early assessment of the age of baobabs, see M. Adanson, "Description d'un arbre d'un nouveau genre appelé Baobab, observé au Sénégal," *Mémoires de l'Académie Royale des Sciences* (1761), 218–243, and Carl Ludwig Willdenow, *Grundriss der Kräuterkunde* (Berlin: Haude and Spener, 1792), 292.

13–Mielck, *Die Riesen*, 5.

14–Achille Richard, *Nouveaux éléments de botanique et de physiologie végétale* (Paris: Béchet Jeune, 1822), 97–99; Mr. de Candolle, *Notice sur la longévité des arbres et les moyens de la constater* (Bibliothèque Universelle, 1831); [Augustin-Pyramus de Candolle], *Mémoires et souvenirs de Augustin-Pyramus de Candolle écrits par lui-même et publiés par son fils* (Geneva: Cherbuliez, 1862), 393, 462, 567–68.

15–Alexander Harvey, *Observations on the Nature, Longevity, and Size of Trees* (Edinburgh: Neill and Company, 1846).

16–Wang et al., "Multifeature analyses of vascular cambial cells reveal longevity mechanisms in old Ginkgo biloba trees," *Proceedings of the National Academies of Science* 117, no. 4 (2020): 2201–2210; Sergi Munné-Bosch, "Limits to Tree Growth and Longevity," *Trends in Plant Science* 23, no. 11 (2018): 985–993.

17–Wang, "Multifeature analyses"; Munné-Bosch, "Limits to Tree Growth"; Mielck, *Die Riesen*, 8.

18–von Burgsdorf, *Versuch einer vollständigen*, 41, plate 1.

19–Gottlob König, "Die Poesie des Waldbaues," *Forstliches Cotta-Album* (Breslau und Oppeln: Graß und Barth, 1844), 139–141; Freiherr v.d. Borch, "Ästhetik im Walde," *Allgemeine Forst- und Jagdzeitung* no. 136 (13. November 1830): 542–543; Freiherr von der Borch, "Die Ästhetik im Walde," *Sylvan: Jahrbuch für Forstmänner Jäger und Jagdfreunde auf das Jahr 1824* (1824): 77–110. Also see Heinrich von Salisch, *Forstästhetik* (Berlin: Julius Springer, 1885), 228. On Gottlieb König and Forstästhetik, see Ekkehard Schwartz, *Lebensbilder bedeutender Forstleute: Gottlob König 1779–1849. Ein Leben für Wald und Landschaft* (Erfurt: Kleinhampl, 1999), 312–315.

20–von Salisch, *Forstästhetik*, 153–155.

21–Haus Wendgräben von Wulffen-Mahndorf, "Beziehungen zwischen Waldbau und Forstästhetik," *Die Gartenkunst* 34, no. 4 (1921): 48–51; Rudolf Goethe, "Bücherschau: Forstästhetik," *Die Gartenkunst* 4, no. 6 (1902): 119–120; Rudolf Goethe, "Bücherschau: Forstästhetik," *Die Gartenkunst* 7, no. 2 (1905): 31–33; Schier, "Landesverschönerung und Heimatschutz: Waldästhetik," *Die Gartenkunst* 6, no. 12 (1904): 223–225.

22–Sonja Dümpelmann, *Seeing Trees: A History of Street Trees in New York City and Berlin* (New Haven and London: Yale University Press, 2019), 47–48; A. Chargueraud, *Les arbres de la ville de Paris. Traité des Plantations dans les villes et sur les routes départementales* (Paris: J. Rothschild, 1896), 265–266.

23–Victor Buchholz, "'Der Fächerbaum' Ginkgo biloba L. als Straßenbaum," *Gartenflora* 81, no. 10 (1932): 241–244.

24–Joseph Stübben, *Der Städtebau, 9. Halb-Band des Handbuches der Architektur, Vierter Teil* (Darmstadt: Arnold Bergsträsser, 1890), 441–42. For interplanting, also see Sonja Dümpelmann, "Trees, Wood, and Paper: Materialities of Urban Arboriculture in Modern Berlin," *Journal of Urban History* 46, no. 2 (2020): 310–333.

25–The paragraphs on Chicago are adopted and adapted from Dümpelmann, "'Tree Doctor' vs. 'Tree Butcher': Material Practices and Politics of Arboriculture in Chicago," in *Landscript 05: Material Culture*, ed. Jane Hutton (Berlin: Jovis, 2017), 90–113.

26–Stewart cited in Dümpelmann, "'Tree Doctor,'" 90–113.

27–See the adjective "leafy," in *Oxford English Dictionary* online, accessed October 25, 2024, https://www.oed.com/dictionary

28–Mariya Shcheglovitova, "Valuing Plants in Devalued Spaces: Caring for Baltimore's Street Trees," *Nature and Space* 3, no. 1 (2020): 228–245. Also see Anastasia Loukaitou-Sideris and Renia Ehrenfeucht, *Sidewalks: Conflict and Negotiation over Public Space* (Cambridge, MA: The MIT Press, 2009), 203.

29–On women's work and philanthropy, see Kathleen D. McCarthy, "Women and Political Culture" in *Charity, Philanthropy, and Civility in American History*, eds. Lawrence J. Friedman and Mark D. McGarvie (Cambridge: Cambridge University Press, 2002), 179–198.

30–Dümpelmann, *Seeing Trees*, 97–122.

31–Dümpelmann, *Seeing Trees*, 186–217; Sonja Dümpelmann, "Occupying Public Space, Generating Public Spheres: Street Tree Art and Activism in East and West Berlin in the 1970s and 1980s," in *The Politics of Street Trees*, eds. Camilla Allen and Jan Woudstra (London: Routledge, 2022), 291–306.

32–This paragraph is adapted from Sonja Dümpelmann, "Planting, Pruning, Picking: The Politics and Art of Urban Tree Care," in *Climate Bridge: An International Perspective on How to Enact Climate Action at the Government Public Interface*, eds. Wolfram Höfer, Sebastian Schlecht, Frank Gallagher, Arianna Lindberg, and Angela Oberg (New Brunswick: Rutgers University Press, 2025).

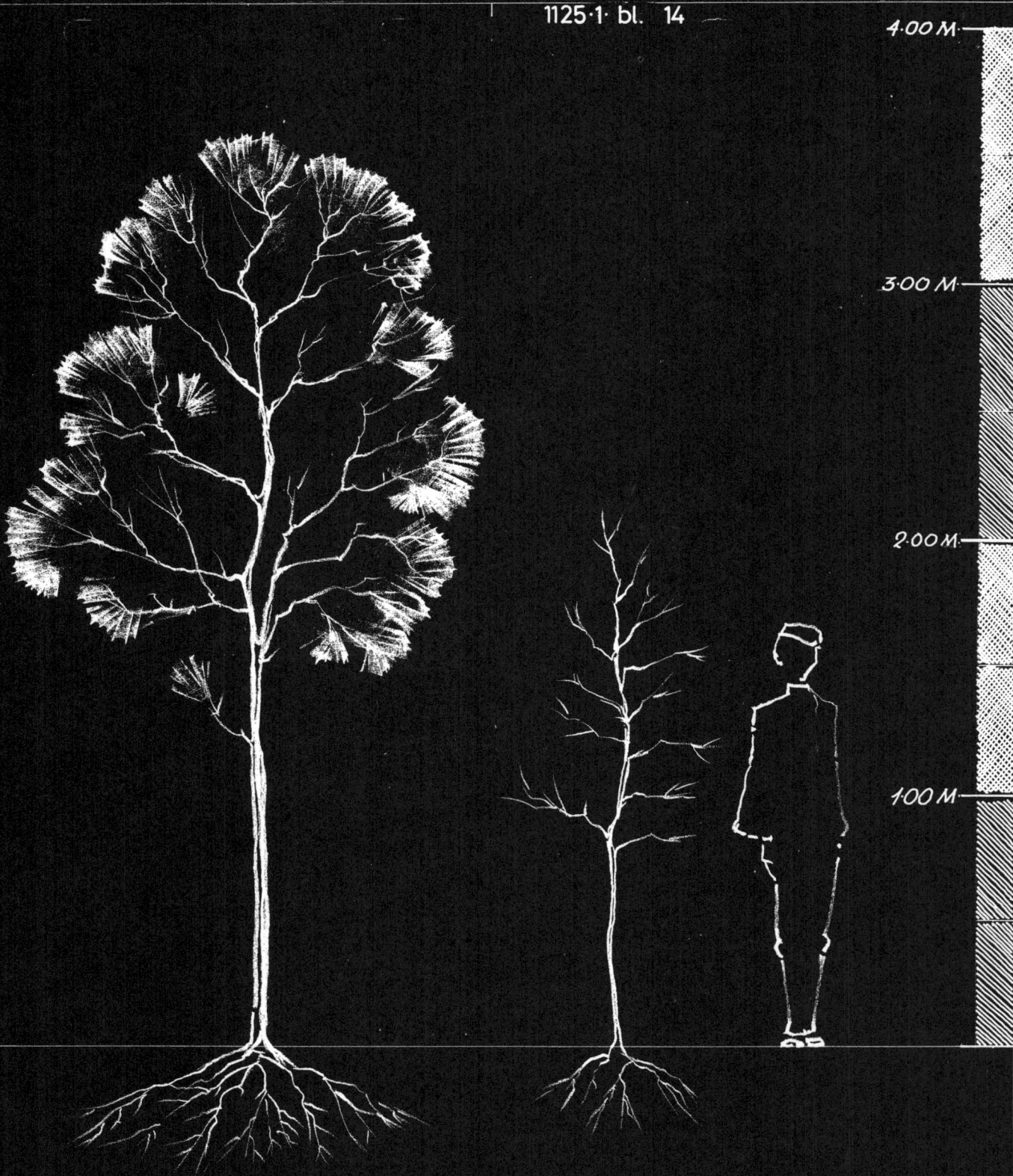

Noël van Dooren

TREES FOLLOW DRAWINGS, DRAWINGS FOLLOW TREES

In this essay Noël van Dooren explores the importance of time in landscape, the role of design drawings, and the specific position of trees as a crucial landscape ingredient.

PART ONE

It is about drawings I want to speak here, more precisely, design drawings. The invention and the making of new landscapes is the larger context. Design drawings are fascinating. They can be seen as mere instruments in the production of landscapes. They are also objects in themselves, evoking landscapes in their possible future realities, but also having their own beauty, logic, and life. Landscape and drawings will exist as a separate reality—Goffi describes this as the "twinned body."[1] A design for a future reality includes many drawings made in different phases, for different audiences, of different types. Plan, section, visualization, and diagram became known and codified ways to represent the future landscape. But landscape is a rather fluid phenomenon—growing, changing, evolving in expected and unexpected ways. This has always received less attention in drawings.

The question of how to depict time has occupied mankind for ages. Propositions have been made, in cartography, painting, film, and information design.[2] Landscape design drawings have a specific challenge: landscape by default is ongoing. The implicit question for drawings is where we are, in time. The profession did arrive at silent conventions to tackle this. Drawings have an ambiguous position in time. Expertise on the time aspects of landscape is seen as embodied knowledge that does not necessarily have to be made explicit.[3] That refers to the roles that drawings have in design processes. They can be a laboratory to further explore emerging design ideas by the designer. Drawings also are the instruments to hand over design ideas to clients and the larger public. Apparently, time issues are not seen as very important—adequate information in landscape design presentations is rare. And drawings also are the vehicles to instruct the making. How to manage the realized design to arrive at desired future states? In general, the management phase is outside the designers' influence. That is felt as unsatisfactory as in landscape making, becoming, developing, and managing are overlapping.

Despite the fluid nature of landscape, the issue of time has not been addressed thoroughly in the history of landscape architecture. However, three pivotal contributions explicitly reflected on the issue and tested out options. The first is the work of nineteenth-century "landscape gardener" Humphry Repton, who invented "before and after" drawings—technically the first "time drawings" in landscape architecture.[4] The second is Lawrence Halprin, whose *RSVP Cycles* and his drawings are seminal in this field.[5] The third is James Corner, one of the front men of landscape urbanism, particularly with his writings.[6]

Trees have a crucial position in this argument. As the iconic building blocks of landscapes, they are the living examples of time "at work." Trees of twenty to thirty years may be of a certain size, but they still are in their puberty. Only at eighty years and older are trees adult, and they easily can live for centuries. Trees therefore are also central characters in landscape architecture drawing. Following conventions in legends, a circle often stands for a tree, and if a scale is given, this also indicates a size. Size however unavoidably refers to time, as a certain size counts for a given time frame. The newly planted tree only is the opening move of the landscape game. Often, the circle is silently understood as an estimation of the growth after twenty to thirty years. Further in time, the circle is "outgrown" by the tree—reality escapes the design drawing. Landscape design drawings therefore stand for a future landscape and at the same time neglect fundamental characteristics of landscape. The tree is both a telling example and a metaphor, as we could broaden the discourse to many aspects of landscape. The flowering of gardens is an easy example but think also of the large-scale landscape mechanisms of flooding, erosion, succession. The returning idea is change, dynamics, and tendency.

Speaking about time and dynamics, we first have to see the basic distinction between circular and progressive time.[7] The tree is the perfect example of progressive time. The mechanism of ebb and flood is obviously circular. Note that reality is more complex: the daily circularity of ebb and flood is influenced by moon rhythms and larger cycles. Seasonality as an example of circularity also defines the tree but seasonality develops over time; only the mature fruit tree gives a rich harvest and at old age production declines.

Secondly, we have to note expected change—the growing tree—versus unexpected dynamics, which range from natural events (storms, droughts, sicknesses) to human forces, such as happenings and events. Landscape architects know that such dynamic changes will occur, but not when, where, and how often. Designs have to be prepared. Finally, narrational time has its own position; in stories and film time speeds up or is rewound. In such a cultural perspective, meanings and understandings shift over time, which, for trees, can be clearly seen.

Drawings have different types, roles, materials, and messages.[8] Drawing types as derived from the architectural tradition do not show time aspects per se but can do so when presented in series or related to specific moments. Diagrams offer more possibilities, and newly introduced drawing types such as the score allow a focus on time. A fundamental shift made in the score is the attention to *who* is doing something to reach a future state, and *when* that is done, as crucial additions to the *what* and the *where* that plan and section deliver. Drawings can be analytical, observing time processes at work in landscape, or speculative. Perhaps the most important is how far drawings reveal the mechanism at work, and what graphical solutions are found to do so.

PART 2—DRAWINGS AND CAPTIONS

*Score for Sea Ranch.
Lawrence Halprin, 1968*

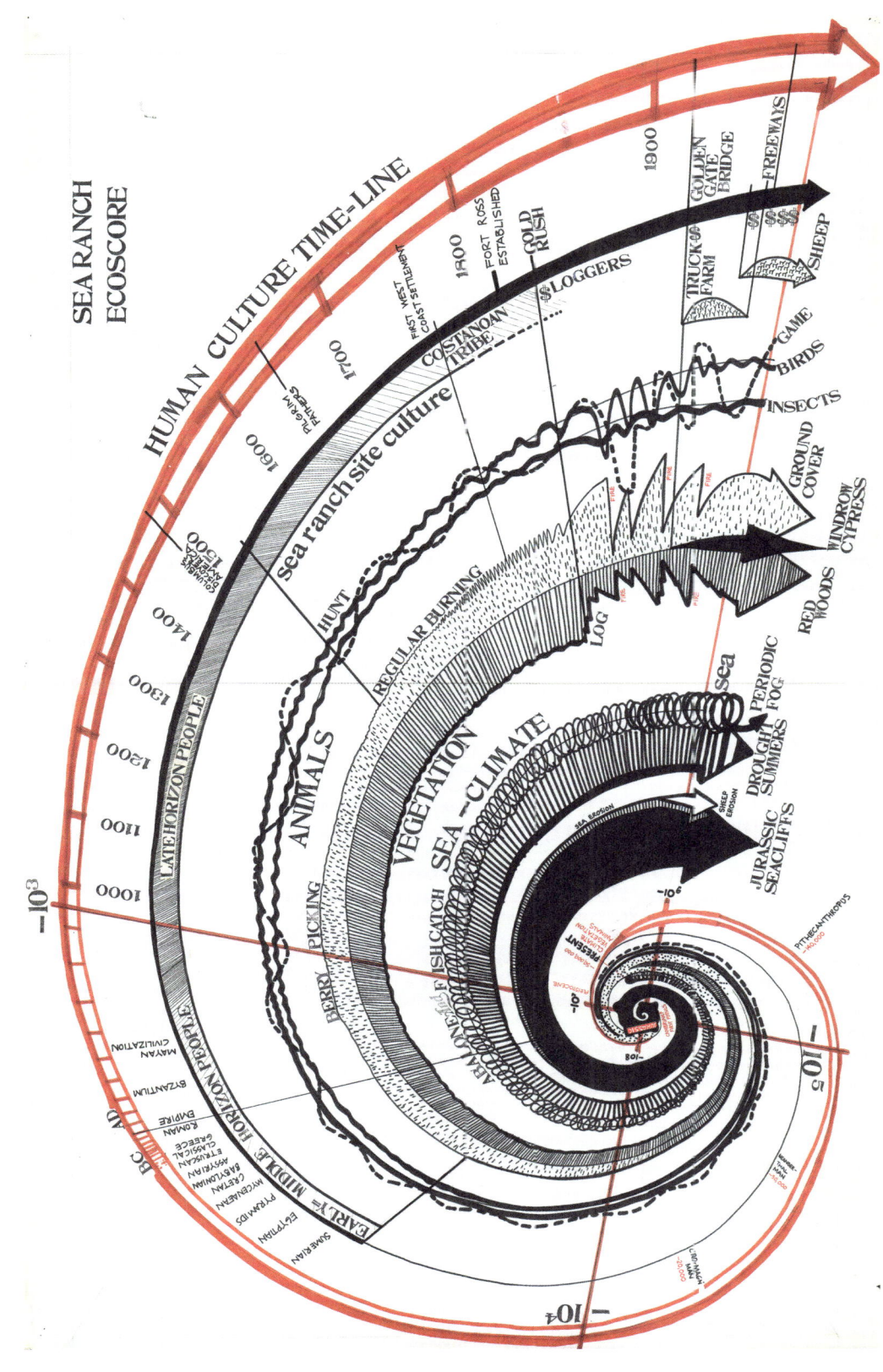

Halprin developed this "ecoscore" for the Sea Ranch project in Sonoma, California. From 1962 onwards, a new village was planned in close relation to the landscape. The project became iconic. Halprin's significance is also in introducing the score to landscape architecture. Inspired by his wife, choreographer Ann Halprin, he explored the options of the score both as a means for analysis and a design tool. Graphically, scores have many forms. Here the spiral set-up is chosen to show the sped-up development of landscape over time and the growing influence of man. The score has not become a mainstream drawing type in landscape architecture so far; however, it has not lost its actuality as a proposition for representing time.

Section or profile diagram of two moments in time, Oxhagen stand.
Roland Gustavsson, Swedish University of Agricultural Science,
1983 and 1993

Inspired by Paul Richards's 1952 *The tropical rainforest,* Gustavsson draws "profile diagrams" as observational studies of existing plantations. In the architecture tradition, these drawings can be seen as sections, which points at their parallel generic and specific description of forests. They are notational strategies to display the development of plantations, overcoming our assumptions of tree growth and carefully observing reality as it is. How trees are shaped expresses their growth history. These profile diagrams are "a snapshot of a moment in time in the evolution of a landscape"—creating space to discuss potential future development. By revisiting the drawn situation, these sections record development over time. Despite technological progress, today this is still done by hand to "slow down" and to reach the embodied understanding of how (designed) forests operate.[9]

32

Diagram for the Lace Garden.
Anouk Vogel, The Netherlands, 2009

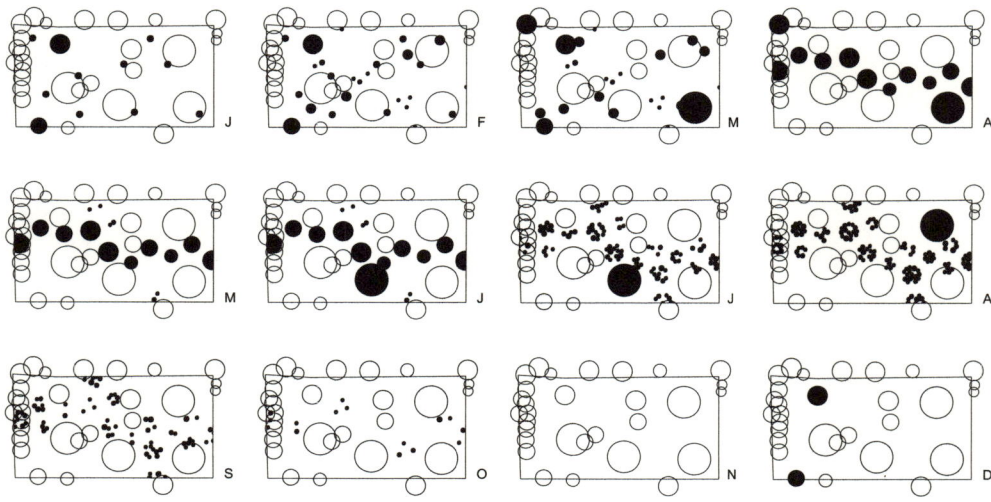

The Lace Garden was realized in Amsterdam in 2009. This diagram displays the flowering of a garden over months. In the first version, colors were used to represent the actual flowering, but in the final drawing this was reduced to yes or no, translated in black and white. That underlines the aesthetic considerations in making a drawing and choices regarding the informational value. An important question is what time scale or what moments in time to choose. Flowering often is understood as a spring and summer phenomenon. As this garden was designed to be relevant throughout the year, a neutral monthly overview was chosen.

*Plan drawing for Højstrup Parken.
C. Th. Sørensen, undated*

This drawing for a green area between residential housing blocks in Odense, Denmark, comments in an implicit-yet-essential way on the time aspect of landscape. Sørensen had a nursery background and was very aware of how to arrive at beautiful mature oaks, such as the thirty-two planned here. The drawing is strikingly ambiguous. It seems to suggest these thirty-two trees, but in fact circles were made, and per circle, twenty to thirty saplings were planted. Over the years the young trees were thinned. Photographs made over the years give an insight into how the design developed.[10]

*Plan drawing for Greenwich Millennium Park.
Michel Desvigne Paysagiste, landscape architects, France, 2000*

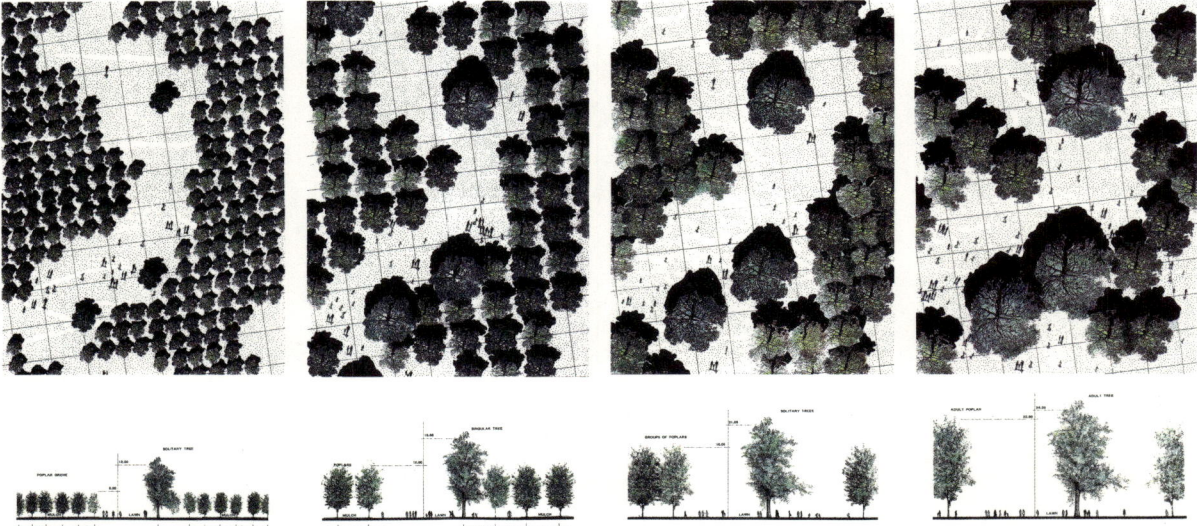

Millennium Park was realized in London in 2000. This plan drawing shows the evolution of the design in four points in time. The drawing combines both plan and section in a series of four. As the moments are not specified, it can be considered an abstraction of the evolution of time. In a discourse on drawing time, this is an iconic example for its implicit statement by a well-known designer that a design for a green public space cannot be represented in terms of one final state. This specific drawing does not expand on how one state transgresses to the other, illustrating the fact that a design drawing is both an individual object and part of a larger package.[11]

34

*Sectional diagram.
Johanna Bendlin, 2020*

Afforestation is a very interesting theme in this context, as it combines the cultural act of planting, the role of management, and the knowledge of succession. Bendlin proposes a large afforestation of the low-lying southern Denmark meltwater floodplains, threatened by rising sea levels. This supports the Danish aim to increase forested land, and Bendlin's goal to reconnect with the soil and to create a more adaptive system. The attention to the soil is reflected in the sectional diagram that treats "above" equally with "beneath." Reading from left to right, time progresses from five to a hundred years. Also, complexity progresses: we see how the system develops a balance between decay and rejuvenation, supported by a root system that also in the drawing becomes a larger whole.[12]

Mixed drawing for Insel Hombroich and photographs of the intervention at the Bruecke Museum.
Atelier Le Balto, 2022/2021–2024

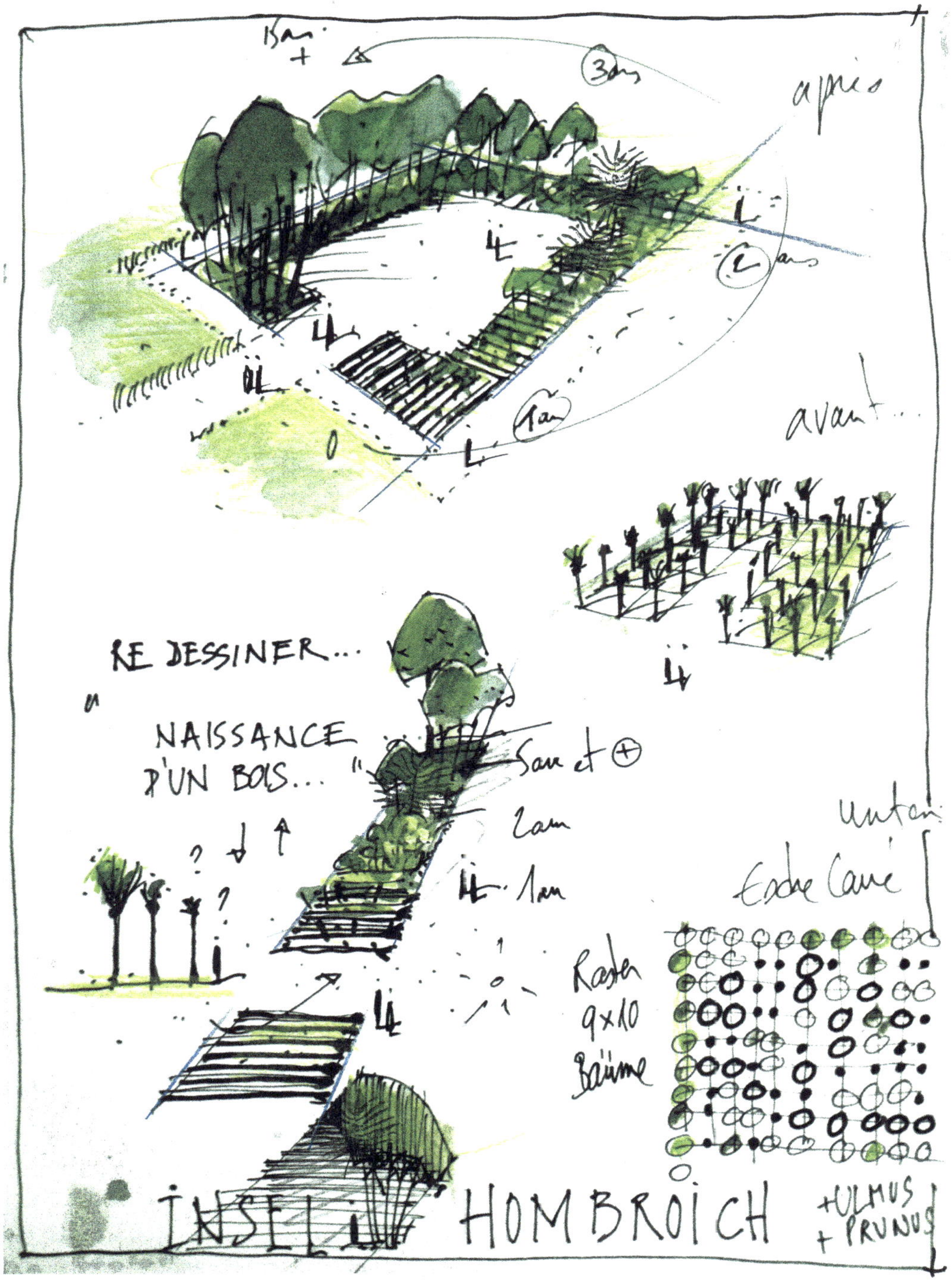

Two image types and two projects are combined as they add up. Le Balto works at the art museum Insel Hombroich without ready design drawings. Quick sketches function as instructions for "actions weeks." The drawing describes the initial situation, the action, the result. Over time, the effect of earlier actions is evaluated and continued with new actions. The plan grows with the garden, as put by the client. This drawing suggests cutting down an infected *Fraxinus* stand and to use the felled ashes for a new development to support biodiversity and as a clear design intervention. The photographs document more or less the same technique to create—after taking down the fence—a natural closure of the garden at the Bruecke Museum.

PART 3

Trees follow drawings, drawings follow trees. As far as landscape is a play, the work of a landscape architect is to do an opening move. Land is prepared, trees are planted, conditions are given for nature to take over. To some extent the landscape fulfills over time the promise in the drawing. But landscapes also outgrow the drawing. How far does the designer follow the landscape, redrawing and updating the next steps? A crucial issue in drawing time is the clarity about what mechanisms are at work. That understanding is also its contribution to design education: what forces are shaping the landscape over time, and how exactly are they acting. That awareness allows the landscape architect to choose specific representational types, drawing materials, and the relevant moments in time.

Playing the devil's advocate: are drawings necessary to understand time in landscape? The irony is that the designer's dialogue with time can be translated in being present, responding, acting at the spot in a continuous conversation with the landscape at hand. In the selection of drawings here, the work of Atelier Le Balto shows how a designer can be present in the landscape, and how design can shift to instructions and registrations. In the complex world of clients, budgets, permits, and contracts, however, the landscape architect may not be on site to engage with the developing design. All relevant instructions have to be handed over; a promise of a future landscape has to be made. Acting in a tight legal and economical space, explicitly showing time aspects may even be considered dangerous, as it would reveal how fragile many bold landscape statements are.

At the same time, in a world in which the dynamic forces of nature seem to be more present than ever—severe droughts, storms, floods and fires—an approach of future landscapes that is rooted in expertise on the forces at work seems urgent. Equally, it seems relevant today that landscape architects take responsibility to inform society of the risks and hazards of landscape futures; even better, they should try to engage the public in understanding these dynamics as the beauty of landscape.

Many of the challenges society faces today relate to the urban and rural landscape. Climate, food, soil, biodiversity, and identity pose major questions. These questions cross with cultural, political, and economic issues such as migration and inequality. Particularly for its inherent relationship with change and dynamics, landscape architecture seems well-equipped to engage in such issues; and time drawings are key to explore, communicate, and deal with dynamism.

Trees are both active and passive partners in the dynamic times we live in. They literally shape a better climate in densifying cities, provide a living for a large array of other beings, are in dialogue with the soil, create water storage, and help people to anchor in place and time. But to do so, an offensive approach is needed. We need many, many more trees, we need adaptive species, we need trees in species-rich ensembles, we need trees that will mature and enfold themselves for decades, centuries. To realize that in the contemporary dynamic (urban) landscape is a huge task.

Bottom-line, it is a flaw in landscape architecture theory that the representation of time has been embraced so late and so weakly, but new generations can be equipped with adequate knowledge, examples, and thinking about drawing time. If it were a tree, it did grow slowly, but it finally reached maturity and we now only can wish it will stay here for centuries, healthy, inspired, and fruit-bearing.

1– As described in Federica Goffi, "Architecture's twinned body: building and drawing," in *From Models to Drawings: Imagination and Representation in Architecture*, eds. Marco Frascari, Jonathan Hale, and Bradley Starkey (Nottingham: University of Nottingham, 2007), 88–98.

2– See Daniel Rosenberg and Anthony Grafton, *Cartographies of Time: A History of the Timeline*, 2010, and Edward Tufte, *Envisioning Information*, 1990.

3– Noël Van Dooren, *Drawing Time: The Representation of Change and Dynamics in Dutch Landscape Architectural Practice after 1985*, 2017.

4– See John C. Loudon (ed.), *The Landscape Gardening and Landscape Architecture of the Late Humphrey Repton ESQ*, 1840/1988.

5– See Lawrence Halprin, *The RSVP Cycles: Creative Processes in the Human Environment*, 1969.

6– See James Corner, "Representation and Landscape," 1992; Charles Waldheim (ed.), *The Landscape Urbanism Reader*, 2006.

7– See Eviatar Zerubavel, *Time Maps*, 2003. See also The Long Now Foundation, https://media.longnow.org/files/2/LongNowDiag.jpg.

8– Eve Blau and Edward Kaufman (eds.), *Architecture and Its Image: Four Centuries of Architectural Representation* (1989) is instructive, as is Erik de Jong, Michel Lafaille, and Christian Bertram, *Landscapes of the Imagination* (2008).

9– See Anders Busse Nielsen, Lisa Diedrich, and Catherine Szanto, *Woods Go Urban: Landscape Laboratories in Scandinavia*, 2023.

10– Carl Theodor Sørensen reflects on his work in *Haver: Tanker og arbejder*, 1975. See for a "drawing experiment," Noël van Dooren and Anders Busse Nielsen, "The Representation of Time: Addressing a Theoretical Flaw in Landscape Architecture," in *Landscape Research 44*, no. 8 (2018): 997–1013, DOI:10.1080/01426397.2018.1549655.

11– See Gilles A. Tiberghien, *Intermediate Natures: The Landscapes of Michel Desvigne*, 2009.

12– See Johanna Bendlin, *Growing Horizons: Investigations of Soil and the Underground*, 2020.

Fig 1 White Ash Snowshoe, watercolor-photo collage, Samantha Jamero, 2023.
Collage features Eastern Woodland narrow, pointed Ojibwe snowshoes and Cree Montagnais/Innu snowshoes

Jana VanderGoot

US EASTERN WOODLANDS ASH, TAKE CARE

The case study project in this essay is about humans and forests as relatives who take each other to heart. The work acknowledges that humans breathe because the forest has been breathing for a very long time. Rico Newman—a Choptico Band Piscataway-Conoy Tribe of Maryland elder—reminded the project team that humans are younger relatives of trees. Kelly Church—Match-e-benash-she-wish Potawatomi/Odawa/Ojibwe black ash basket-maker, fiber artist, educator, activist and culture keeper—taught the team about Black ash—human kinship. Dr Shelbi Nahwilet Meissner—Luiseño and Cupeño assistant professor at the University of Maryland and director of the Indigenous Futures Lab—built caretaking coalitions with blanketing, basketmaking, beading, singing, weaving, and writing. Architectural designer and researcher Samantha Jamero's hands connected plants, people, and buildings. Jana VanderGoot—architect and associate professor at the University of Maryland—was grateful for space to return to the practice of making alongside the usual writing and teaching about making.

INTRODUCTION: ARCHITECTURE AND THE FOREST AESTHETIC, 2024
by Jana VanderGoot
"We live with the Forest, and we take it to heart." This was the first line of the book, *Architecture and the Forest Aesthetic*, published in 2017. There were several reactions to that introduction, but landscape architect Elizabeth Meyer, who wrote the foreword, offered a response that stood out among others. She strategically placed *Architecture and the Forest Aesthetic* in a practical and academic context, but she also shared how she felt and what she thought about the forest by her home. She welcomed the most basic message of the book and responded in kind.

In a book review titled, "Model, Medium, and Metaphor: Planning and Design Confront the Natural World," Meredith Drake Reitan pointed out what was missing from *Architecture and the Forest Aesthetic* and other works on landscape architecture and biophilic design published between 2016 and 2020. The texts did not attend to "the extensive literature of nature human interactions found in cultural geography."[1]

Well-known American geographer Carl O. Sauer introduced the term "cultural landscapes" in 1925: "Culture is the agent, the natural area is the medium, the cultural landscape is the result." Sauer advocated for a land ethic, responsible stewardship, and decentering the human voice, and yet Sauer's definition describes a world where culture is centered as active—alive—and nature, an area, is not recognized that way.[2]

While the definition of cultural landscapes has expanded since 1925 to take on new meanings, it still often describes landscape as an object, a medium, or a place, as it does in the language of the UNESCO heritage and the US National Park websites. If I could go back to *Architecture and the Forest Aesthetic*, I would revise the first sentence to this: *We live with the Forest, and we take it to heart. The Forest is breathing rather than a place to breathe.* I would also add more temperate-forest-biome case study projects, as featured in the essay below, to represent this way of being in the world.

US EASTERN WOODLANDS ASH, TAKE CARE by Kelly Church, Samantha Jamero, Shelbi Nahwilet Meissner, Rico Newman, and Jana VanderGoot
The *Ash, Take Care* project pokes holes in the architectural Design Thinking process, as articulated by the Hasso-Plattner Institute, which involves Understanding, Contextualizing, Defining a Point of View, Ideating, Prototyping, and Testing, but not always in that order.[3] When the *Ash, Take Care* project team focused their attention on participatory action research to prioritize historical and cultural research methodologies, the group could see more clearly how architectural design thinking often runs the risk of cultural appropriation. In addition, bringing *Making as Knowing* research methods—as described by Pamela Smith—to the design thinking process highlighted the importance in an academic setting of acknowledging limits of knowledge and working in parallel tracks of allyship.

TREE STORIES AS DESIGN THINKING
In 2023, an architecture design studio at the University of Maryland, College Park, met with Rico Newman and other

members of the Piscataway-Conoy and Nanticoke Indian tribes to share tree stories. The event officially commenced a semester-long project of mutual learning and exploration of the diverse epistemologies and practices involved in working with trees to co-create wooden objects. Fifteen students crafted collages as gifts to foster deeper connections between project participants and highlight the cultural significance of the work. Tree stories offered as spoken word by Indigenous participants represented worldviews unfamiliar to the students. For instance, the students needed time to process what Rico Newman meant when he referred to trees as "one-legged."

Samantha Jamero shared a collage, *White Ash Snowshoe,* in response to reading the Ojibwe language dictionary. Simple linguistic analysis of words shed light on the links between wood craft and plant relatives. White ash, *aagimaak* (*Fraxinus americana*), is a tree with hard, durable wood traditionally used for making snowshoe frames. In Ojibwe, terms for "snowshoe" and "white ash stem" are connected. *Aagim* in the word for white ash translates to snowshoe. In a verb phrase, *bimaagimose//* "s/he [they] snowshoes along or by, goes snowshoeing," white ash is carried in the meaning of snowshoe.[4] Indigenous collaborators noted to the team that the white ash ancestor of the snowshoe is invoked when the word is used, likely reminding Ojibwe people of responsibilities and relationships to their tree relatives (Fig 1).

BLACK ASH BASKETMAKING AS DESIGN THINKING

The project team participated in a basketmaking workshop with Kelly Church, an artist, educator, culture keeper, and Pottawatomi/Ottawa/Ojibwe basketmaker enrolled in the Match-E-Be-Nash-She-Wish Band. Church provided splints of black ash tree (*Fraxinus nigra*)—*wisgak* and *bapagakw'egen* and *bapagakw'egnatek* in Potawatomi.[5] Church's family together prepared these thin, ribbon-like strips of wood. Sharing this work is an important part of their tradition.

While weaving, Church shared a story of her ancestors' kinship with black ash. The story extends to the present as her family brings awareness to the loss of ash stands due to the emerald ash borer (EAB) (*Agrilus planipennis*) insect. The US Forest Service considers EAB to be an invasive species, and the presence of EAB in a tree means it will likely die within three years. Ash populations have declined by tens of millions of trees in the states where the insect has been found (Fig 2).[6]

Church's *Sustaining Traditions—Digital Memories* basket at the US Smithsonian Museum offers a socio-ecological perspective on the EAB. Impacts affect basketmakers, contribute to wildlife habitat loss, and raise water tables in black ash wetlands. Black ash basketry knowledge includes technical skills required to prepare wood splints and weave baskets in addition to the cultural practice of tracking ecological and climate impacts seven generations into the future. Now that the EAB is part of black ash ecosystems, Church's family seeks to normalize kinship practices like watching for signs of infestation, managing tree harvests to encourage mixed-age growth, collecting seeds, and replanting trees.

DESIGN THINKING AS MAKING

Black ash basketmaking inspired the architecture studio to ask questions:

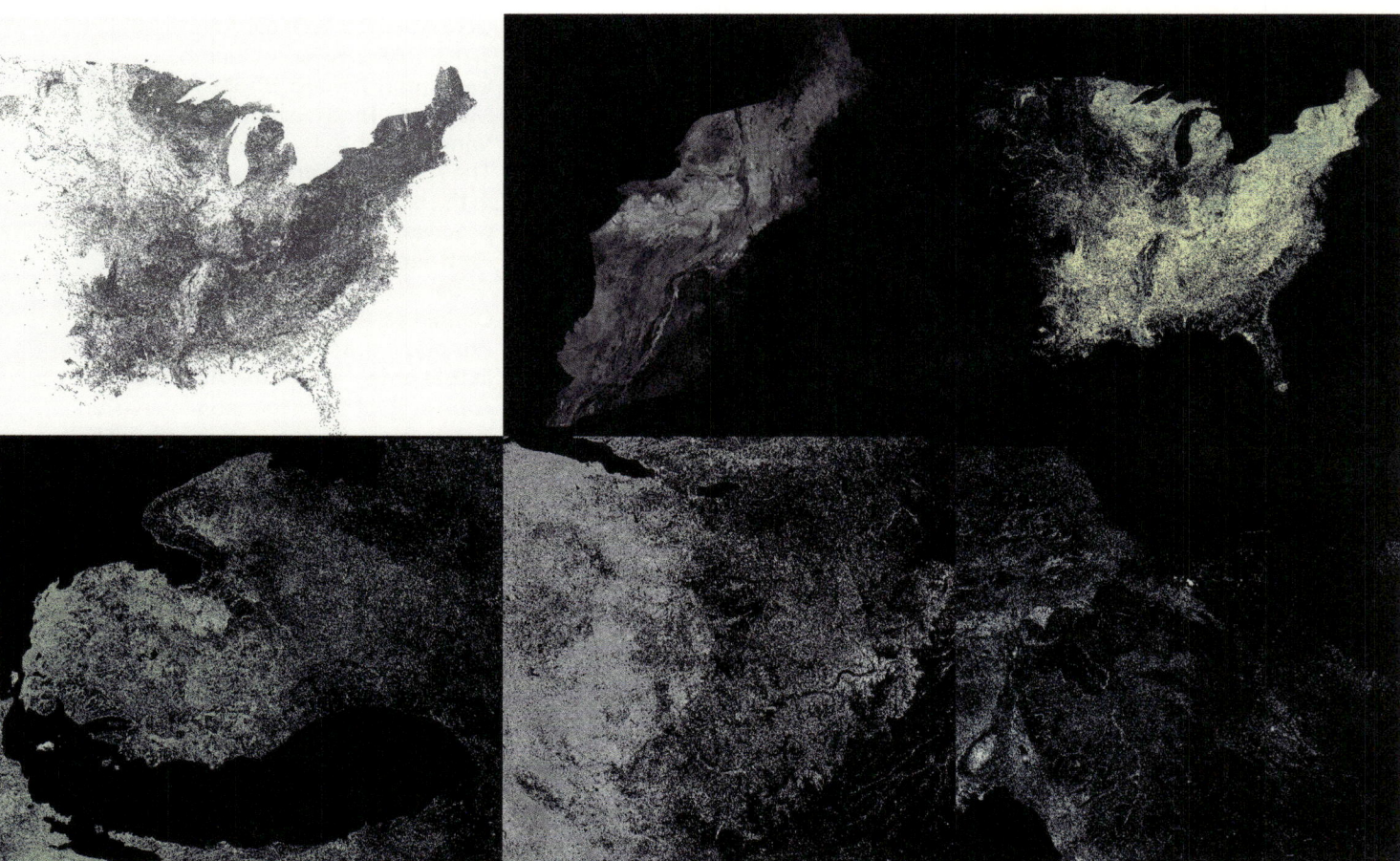

Fig 2 US Eastern Woodlands Ash Tree Footprint, Jana VanderGoot, 2024. Dataset: Live tree basal area (square feet/acre) for all ash species combined (*Fraxinus* spp.) and black ash (*Fraxinus nigra*). B.T. Wilson et al, 2013. Live tree species basal area of the contiguous US (2000–2009). Newtown Square, PA: USDA Forest Service, Rocky Mountain Research Station.

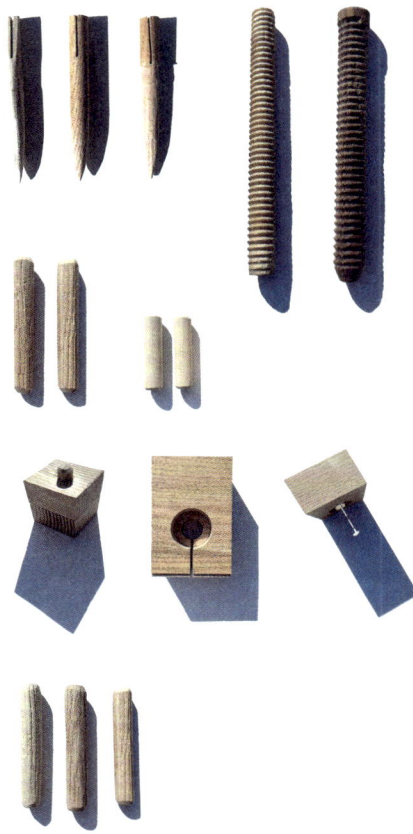

Fig 3   Fire-hardened nails, threaded bolts, grooved dowels, and dowel jig by Chayaporn Pipatpongsa, Jose Gomez, and Zeynep Demircan, 2023

How do craft techniques afford distinct ways of relating to plants? Who can be in the right relation to particular plant relatives to effect ethical relationship building? How might ash continue to have a presence in forests? Could those forests take the form of new crafts, buildings, or even cities?

The studio spent several months using the design thinking process to reflect on those questions in the context of wood-building construction and forest management. The team prioritized the consensus reached through iterative cycles of making and feedback from local community members, professors, and architecture practitioners.

One making activity involved fabricating all-wood fasteners for mass-timber building panels with hand tools, custom jigs, drill presses, and table saw equipment. Observations were made about the behavior of wood types (ash, poplar, oak, pine, fir, and cedar) from one fastener to the next. Reviewers in the feedback sessions appreciated the small wood fasteners are an innovative product that could be made from trees with ash borer activity in the outer layers of the trunk. These trees do not work for baskets or dimensional lumber. Wood fasteners could be a locally sourced, impact-resistant alternative for hardwood nails, dowels, and bolts in all-wood-fastened mass timber. In the US, beech fasteners for mass-timber fabrication are imported from Europe (Fig 3).

Another hands-on activity involved creating wall and roof panels with thin plies of ash and other wood. Although it does not separate the wood along growth rings, rotary cutting to create plywood veneers lowers sawmill wood waste because more of the log is used compared to orthogonal cuts for lumber. The pliability of certain types of wood, including ash, makes them suitable for panels fastened by folding, bending, tabbing, and binding. These techniques present viable alternatives to high-embodied-energy metal nails and glue adhesives, where delamination, chemical off-gassing, and attraction of bacteria and fungi are concerns.

Team members visited *This Present Moment: Crafting a Better World*, 2022 at the Smithsonian American Art Museum's Renwick Gallery in Washington, DC, where baskets incorporated crossed and folded plant fibers in diverse ways. Many ash basket foundations featured two splints crisscrossed at a 90-degree angle. This detail recalled moments in wood-building construction where lengths of wood are fastened together at angles to balance structural strength and rates of building expansion and contraction due to moisture gain and loss. Wood is particularly strong in the direction of its "grain," or parallel to the long lines that tree cells make as they grow up to the sky and down to the earth. Wood cells that are active in tree forms are also alive in building forms (Fig 4).

The design studio activities were more than discussed here, but two consensus outcomes emerged: 1) Cross-laminating thin plies of ash could create dimensionally stable mass plywood; and 2) cross-laminated plies could incorporate more diverse folded, woven, tabbed, nailed, bolted, pinned, and stitched connections to reduce the need for synthetic glues and metal components (Fig 5).

TAKING CARE OF ASH AS DESIGN THINKING

After the architecture studio, the team felt it was important to pause and consider that the brief consultation with Indigenous community members and other diverse stakeholders did not constitute accessing or implementing their knowledge. Indigenous knowledge represents a way of being and relating to the world, with governance value that cannot be separated from Indigenous worldviews and simply integrated into standardized methods. This acknowledgement cast new light on the consensus items and shifted emphasis to the fact that many aspects of wood construction are taken for granted as the only or definitive ways of doing things. Indigenous people and other groups advocating for healthy relationships with the land possess approaches that could balance future practices around wood construction in the North American Eastern Woodlands.

Major obstacles to considering diverse perspectives were elucidated for the team during a double-blind peer review of an article written to share the design studio work. The team was invited to write a piece for a journal focused on sustainability in technology. The authors anticipated feedback about the lack of formula-based structural analysis and numerical data in the submitted manuscript but did

Fig 4   Black ash basket splints in a four-directions pattern from Kelly Church's workshop. Basket by Zeynep Demircan, 2023.

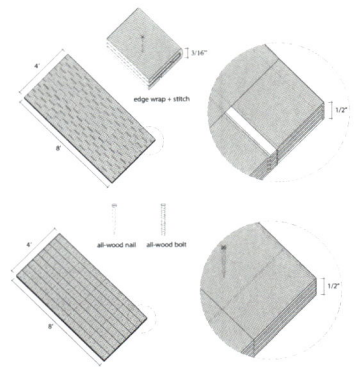

Fig 5   Stacking thin plies with all-wood nails and bolts. Weaving plies with folded, tabbed, and stitched fastening.

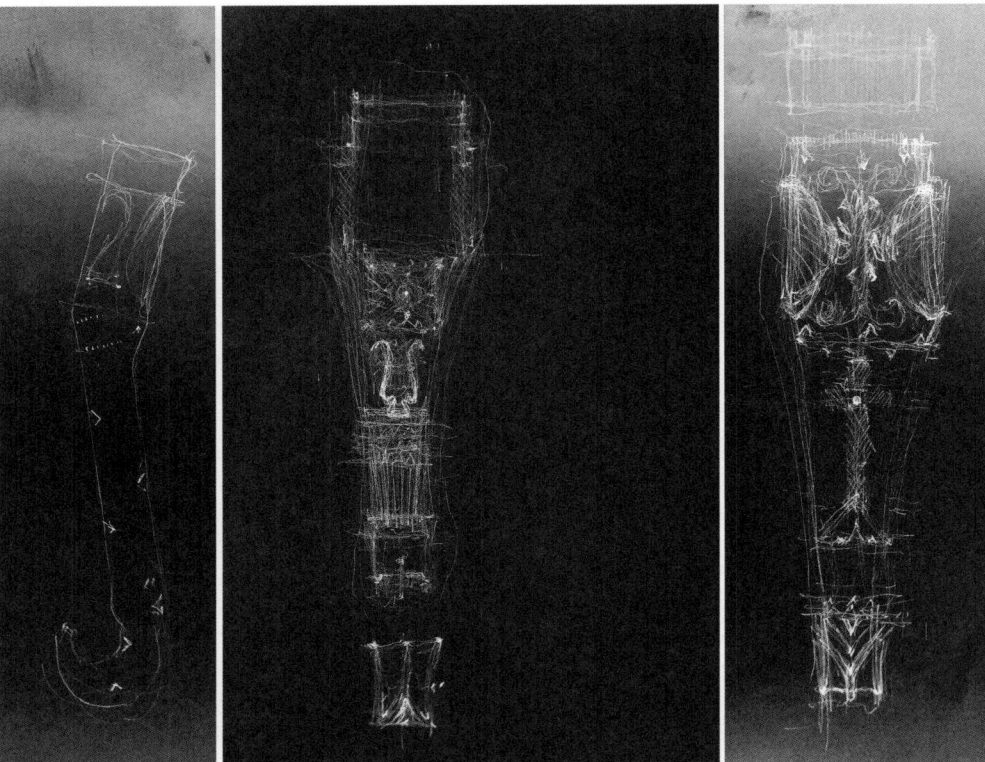

Fig 6 Wood Splint Basket, Jana VanderGoot, 2024. Basket, circa 1880, Daniel Primus (Daniel Primas), Narragansett, ca. 1838-ca. 1890, Rhode Island; US, catalog no. 20/891.

not expect that reviewer comments would so plainly discount the project's cultural significance and interest in sustainable technology forums. Reviewers requested major revisions because the "intellectual merit was compromised," and findings lacked "robustness and vision." It was suggested with certainty that the article "failed to illustrate a single element that shows why stakeholders should select" the building materials described. Another reviewer noted that comparing basketmaking with real-world construction was not relevant. The choice to consider trees from Indigenous communities was discounted with a request to consider Douglas fir, spruce, and pine because they are more common in the construction industry.

Many in academic disciplines of architecture, building construction, and material science would not question the worldview centered in the reviewer comments. Evidence-based science is commonly assumed to be the absolute measure of validity. In "Felt Theory: An Indigenous Approach to Affect and History," Dian Million argues that "academia repetitively produces gatekeepers" that shut out important cultural and social conversations considered to be too heavily validated by feelings. She writes, "we *feel* our histories as well as think them."[7] Likewise, in his book, *At Work in the Ruins,* Dougald Hine expresses concern that the scientific method has an unquestioned authority to determine what is reasonable. He reminds readers that having common sense is *knowing enough.*[8]

The team was confident about the commonsense consensus reached in the DT process and decided to pivot their energy and visit plant relatives held in the US Smithsonian National Museum of the American Indian's (NMAI) Cultural Resources Center (CRC). A review of archival documents and oral histories during earlier DT activities had highlighted the significance of wood construction in North American Eastern Woodlands cultures and communities. Interacting with close to 100 plant relatives from those communities was focused on respecting them as members of their original communities. Those on the team who were more familiar with cultural practices helped teach about gift-giving, smudging, and speaking names of the plants during each visit. As a parallel track, the architects on the team offered their skills in hand-drawing and paper-model-making as allyship (Fig 6).

In her book, *From Lived Experience to Written Word: Reconstructing Practical Knowledge in the Early Modern World*, Pamela Smith writes about Making-and-Knowing research as trials carried out by a mind guided by trained hands. The process is embodied. Hands and the outcomes of handwork are repositories of information more than language-based descriptions of objects and techniques. Making-and-Knowing was a way for members of the team who were not direct relatives of the plants in the collection to acknowledge the limits of their knowledge while still engaging work in parallel with people like Kelly Church, who have kinship relationships with specific plant relatives in the collection.

From the brief visit, the clearest observations were about the particular of weight of each plant relative, the tension and thickness of the woven ash splints and other plant fibers in the baskets, the dryness—and thus fragility—of the wood, and the complex shadows cast by the baskets and other vessels. Holding the hand tools used for making ash baskets felt incredibly special and is not easily described, except to say that it brought great wonder and deep sadness (Fig 7).

It is with *feeling as thinking* that the team returned to the story of the Eastern Woodlands ash in the time of the emerald ash borer (EAB) and other species in forests during climate change. David Foster's edited volume, *Hemlock: A Forest Giant on the Edge,* chronicles the hemlock (*Tsuga canadensis*) tree and the hemlock wooly adelgid (*Adelges tsugae*) insect at the Harvard Forest. Eastern Woodlands forests have seen many cycles of disruption and change, including chestnut blight fungus (*Cryphonectria parasitica*) that brought the once-abundant American chestnut (*Castanea dentata*) down from US forest canopies. At the Harvard Forest, bones of American chestnuts, very decay-resistant trees, still stand upright, literally cradling hemlock trees in their branches. This kinship is stunning to witness given that most of the chestnuts in their native ranges were considered dead

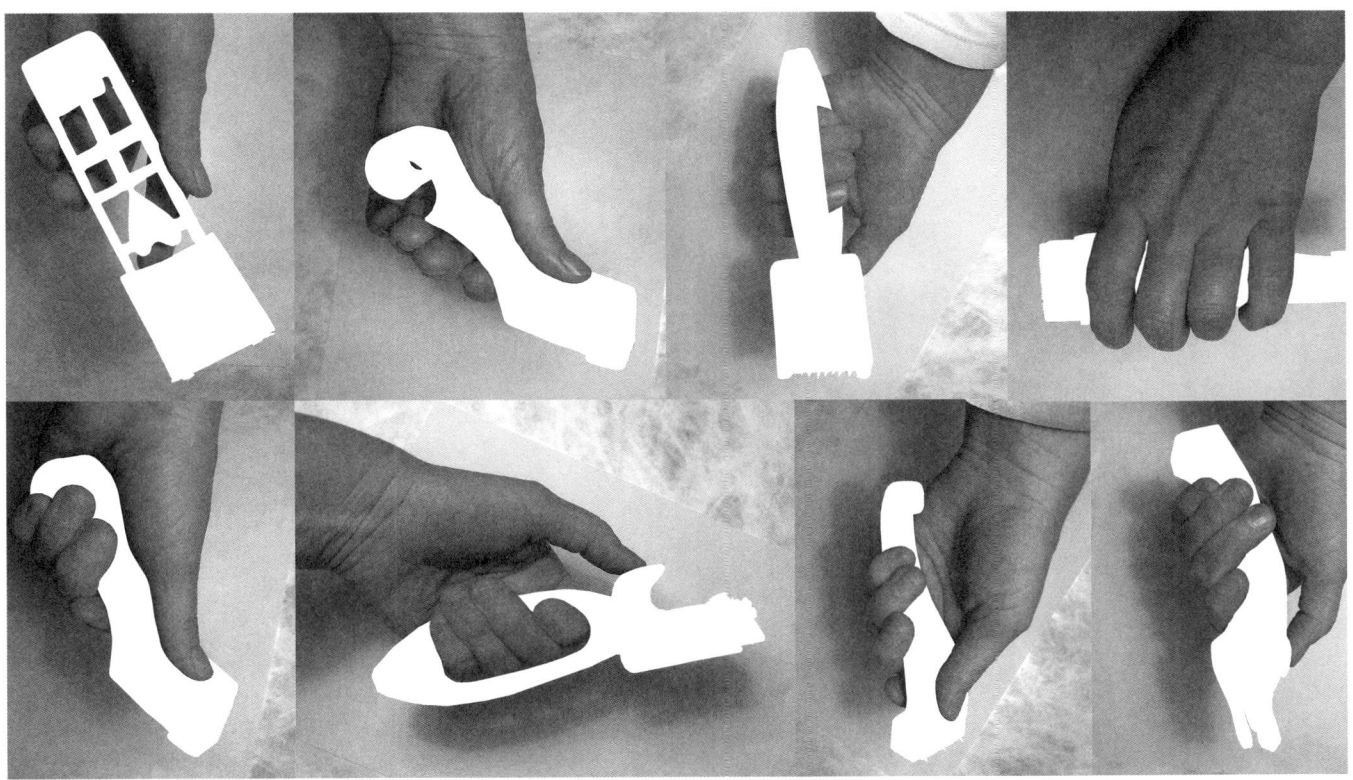

Fig 7 Ash Basketmaking Tools, Jana VanderGoot and Samantha Jamero, 2024. Splint-gauge basketmaking tools from a variety of Eastern Woodlands cultural groups, late 1800s to 1900s.

by 1950.[9] This and other factors led foresters to consider a variety of adelgid management practices, including leaving the adelgid alone.

For ash trees, the EAB signals the end of certain cycles. Are there new and potentially generative cycles that are coming next? What does it mean that the forest hosts the borer? And what lessons are to be learned from taking care during this part of the ash cycle?

ACKNOWLEDGMENTS
A University of Maryland 2022–23 Teaching & Learning Transformation Center grant (Patricia Cossard, principal investigator) supported the design studio course. Authors are thankful for an Association of Collegiate Schools of Architecture (ACSA) 2023 Timber Education Prize Honorable Mention Award. The authors would like to acknowledge the work of the students in addition to the many local community members, professors, and practitioners who offered time in design reviews and hands-on workshops.

A University of Maryland 2024–25 New Directions grant funded work at the US Smithsonian Museum National Museum of the American Indian (NMAI) Cultural Resources Center (CRC). The authors are grateful for CRC staff support during visits.

1–Meredith Drake Reitan, "Model, Medium, and Metaphor: Planning and Design Confront the Natural World," in *Journal of Urban History* 47, no. 1 (2021): 215–222.

2–Carl Ortwin Sauer, *The Morphology of Landscape* (Berkeley: University of California Press, 1925).

3–Hasso-Plattner Institute of Design at Stanford University, accessed October 2024, https://hpi.de/en/school-of-design-thinking/design-thinking/background/design-thinking-process.html.

4–All language translations quoted directly from *The Ojibwe People's Dictionary*, accessed October 20, 2024, www.ojibwe.lib.umn.edu.

5–Cultural Heritage Center, Potawatomi Dictionary, accessed October 2024, https://www.potawatomidictionary.com/Dictionary/Word/321.

6–United States Department of Agriculture and Erica Hupp, "The Future of Ash Trees," accessed February 2024, https://www.fs.usda.gov/about-agency/features/future-ash-trees.

7–Dian Million, "Felt Theory," in *Wicazo Sa Review* 24, no. 2 (2009): 53–76.

8–Dougald Hine, *At Work in the Ruins* (White River Junction, VT: Chelsea Green Publishing, 2023).

9–David R. Foster, ed., *Hemlock: A Forest Giant on the Edge* (New Haven, CT: Yale University Press, 2014).

Laura Leonelli

SHINING HOURS
Women Climbing Trees Tell a Story of Emancipation in Anonymous Photography

Probably the most beautiful definition of what it means to climb a tree, and discover another dimension of oneself, was given by Amy Lowell, the American poet who, starting from her biography, privileged yet conditioned by male will, is a very clear example of an "arboreal woman," a woman who climbs a tree, looks into the distance, grows, makes plans, blossoms. Amy Lowell died one hundred years ago, on May 12, 1925. She was born on February 9, 1874, into one of Boston's wealthiest and most cultured families and yet, when she asked to continue her studies by enrolling at the university, Amy was told no. The text is followed by Laura Leonelli's private collection of anonymous photography.

For a young lady of her rank, it was neither necessary nor appropriate to cross the threshold at Harvard like her brothers—Abbott Lawrence, later president of the university, and Percival, the future astronomer who would discover the existence of the planet Pluto. Tenacious and passionate, Amy Lowell had nevertheless continued to study within the walls of the family library. She traveled, fell in love with Ada Dwyer Russell, and wrote poems dedicated to her. She impressed Ezra Pound with her verse and the year after her death, in 1926, she received the Pulitzer Prize for poetry. One of her most joyful compositions, not surprisingly dedicated to childhood, is entitled "Climbing."[1] The first line is: "High up in the apple tree climbing I go." It was not a random tree that Amy Lowell had climbed, physically and spiritually. The apple tree is the tree of sin, it is the tree sacred to Venus, it is the tree that gives life to the poisoned fruit that the witch offers to Snow White, and it is the tree, legend has it, that suggested the law of gravity to Isaac Newton. For such an abundance of meanings related to love, death, desire, intuition, the apple tree is the tree of true knowledge and of how knowledge transforms us. On an apple tree, *the old apple-tree*, Jo March, the protagonist of *Little Women*, written by Louisa May Alcott in 1864, reads her beloved books.[2] It is an apple tree in which Ingeborg Bachmann, eighteen years old in the summer of 1945, takes refuge, as she tells in her *War Diary*, and among those branches the future writer retains the thrill of her first kiss.[3] And it is an apple tree that Melanie—Angela Carter's fantastic creature and her alter ego in the gothic novel *The Magic Toyshop*, written in 1967—climbs on a stormy night and during her initiation into female adult life, that is, her sexuality.[4]

Why so many emotions when climbing an apple tree, when climbing every tree, in the infinite varieties of these extraordinary living beings? Once more Amy Lowell explains it in the last verse of her poem: "With the sky close above me, the earth far below." Climbing a tree, and one meter of height from the ground is enough, means to enter a personal kingdom, bright and refreshed by the shade, open and protected at the same time, a kingdom in progress between the earth and the sky, where we can also imagine ourselves "in progress." It is as if Virginia Woolf's famous "room of one's own" expanded and, breathing deeply, became "a life of one's own," as psychoanalyst Marion Milner titled her splendid 1934 essay.[5]

Climb a tree, ascend, and once you have reached the right height, look towards the new and wider horizon that opens up before your eyes. Rise, and spread out. The structure of the tree also transforms our psychological structure. Other coordinates, a different height, a diverse base. We could say a different physiognomy, diverse posture. And this "existential novelty" is confirmed through the hundreds and thousands of anonymous photographs that, from 1870 on, portray women on trees in almost every part of the world, or at least in those places where photography became a daily gesture, after George Eastman introduced the first Kodak camera to the market in 1888. The numbers speak for themselves. In 1946 Kodak conducted a survey to evaluate the annual production of amateur photography in the United States. The results were encouraging: one and a half million snapshots. Ten years later, the figure had risen to two billion, and that was because 70 percent of American families now owned a camera.[6] Even just evaluating these two figures, and the exponential, viral growth that the following decades registered, we could say that anonymous photography tells our small, great story better than any other photographic expression. A "skin deep" kind of photograph, the snapshot, the *photographie anonyme*, the vernacular photography, also, in the splendid definition of Thomas Walther, "other pictures."[7] Skin deep because it is like a new skin, a very thin, very sensitive cortex, which records the signs of our time and makes each of us a life in itself, anonymous because unknown, but unique because unrepeatable.

Naturally there are many images of men climbing trees and most of the time the lens captures the muscular effort, the primacy, the courageous ascent to the highest branch. When a woman is photographed in a tree in the front yard, in the vegetable garden behind the house, in a forest, on the shore of a lake, on a beach, in the countryside, in the city, along the road and the car is parked nearby, the story is different, deeper, more radical, because we are talking about uprooting the roots of a destiny to which women have been destined for centuries; that is, the fate of remaining at the foot of a tree and becoming root-women, destined to nourish other existences: fathers, husbands, sons, the eternally free masculine who climbs every tree, looks into the distance, and conquers what he has caught by surprise from that unprecedented height.

Ulysses leaves for his journey, Penelope stays at home and rests on the bed dug by her husband in the trunk of an olive tree. It is perhaps no coincidence that the recognition of the couple occurs precisely around the "immovability" of this tree-bed and the family stability it represents.

This writer began collecting anonymous photography about twenty years ago, and in some ways, it was an emancipation from a gaze that, working as a journalist and curator, had been dedicated almost exclusively to the great authors of photography, mostly men. A gaze that until then had been feminine in the traditional sense, very caring. On the contrary, anonymous photography allows a completely new narrative freedom, a satisfying solitude that feeds on the knowledge gained from the most famous authors, necessary of course, but that at the same time authentically offers the pleasure of a personal reflection, of a journey. In the collection that was taking shape there were very different images. There were only two women in the trees: a tomboy in boots and top hat, smoking a cigarette in the woods; and a double exposure, also taken in the United States at the beginning of the twentieth century. The turning point was first of all the discovery of the volume *Frauen auf Bäumen* by Jochen Raiß.[8] Starting from his important collection of anonymous images, a research project began on the iconographic and literary roots of this unusual figure, which in turn gave birth to the book *Io non scendo. Donne che salgono sugli alberi e guardano lontano*.[9] From the first, it was evident that the women who climb trees disobey the pre-established laws, because climbing a tree means transforming a natural space into a cultural one, an instinctive gesture into a cultural gesture, where culture lies in one's own awareness and where the tools to reach this goal are the cultural and political tools *par excellence*, books. Reading books, writing books, disobeying what is written in some books.

Women who climb trees are insubordinate, and the first to disobey is Eve, who breaks the divine prohibition, approaches the Tree of Knowledge, and eats its fruit. Eve is sin, Eve drags humanity into the abyss of a mortal life. If there is hell, it is her fault, the fault of women. Yet another woman, Margherita Hack, a famous astrophysicist, professor of astronomy at the University of Trieste between 1964 and 1992 and the first woman to direct the Astronomical Observatory in the same city, reads the story of our progenitor differently. Looking into the vastness of that sky that Amy Lowell wrote about, Margherita Hack greets Eve as a sparkling star, as the mother of scientists and philosophers, as the first extraordinary curious person who questions the reality taken for granted. It goes without saying that Margherita Hack, born in 1922, to an antifascist father and a highly cultured mother, did not like the boring games of the good little girls of the time, but preferred to climb the trees in the two gardens that surrounded her house in Ximenes Street, in Florence. By pure coincidence Leonardo Ximenes was a famous astronomer.

The first tree heralding the forest of arboreal women is therefore the one Eve tried to climb, and to pay homage to her we could read her Latin name backwards and greet her like this, *Ave Eva*, as we greet the emperors and the mother of God. Not even the Greco-Roman world, like the biblical one, is particularly appreciative of the transformative communion between trees and female creatures and if it is, deep down, it is a punishment. When Daphne rejects Apollo's embrace, the myth transforms her into a laurel tree, and so Lorenzo Bernini's sculpture surprises her in metamorphosis, "photographic," so instantaneous is it. Daphne is not the only one to find refuge in the remains of a tree. Philyra, seduced by Cronus, transforms into a linden tree; Leuke, pursued by Hades, becomes a white poplar; and Pitis takes the form of a pine tree to escape the violence of Pan. Even Apollo's gesture of placing a laurel wreath on his head can be seen not as a pious homage to his beloved who rejected him and whom he condemned to eternal immobility, but rather a settling of scores. Inspired by the nymphs of the classical world, the Christian world offers the arboreal Madonnas, who miraculously appear seated among branches and leaves, in the act of announcing the birth of a convent or a church near the same tree. If the Virgin holds the Child in her arms and wears a blood-red cloak, if Petrus Christus painted it in 1465, then it is the *Madonna of the Dry Tree*, and the skeletal branches on a black background announce the crown of thorns and the death of the Son who redeems humanity. Once again, the destiny of the woman most venerated by Christianity is the destiny of others, where others are the most blessed of communities, the believers. But when did women climb trees for their own personal "salvation," freeing

Anonymous, *The tree of love*, Ukraine, ca. 1950

Anonymous, Germany, ca. 1950

Anonymous, Unites States, ca. 1910

Anonymous, Ukraine, ca. 1960

Anonymous, United States, ca. 1900

the vocation to the self from every accusation of selfishness and vanity? We have to wait until the nineteenth century, not coincidentally the century in which both photography and a young woman named Jo March were born.

Little Women is the first novel written by a woman, starring female protagonists, targeted at female readers. Evidently such a happy combination had been expected for centuries, so much so that with that novel alone Louisa May Alcott earned $100,000 at the time, equal to about $2,200,000 today. By comparison, Herman Melville (and no one disputes that *Moby Dick* is an absolute masterpiece compared to Alcott's entire production) never exceeded $10,000 in his entire career. The impact of a revolutionary character like Jo is extremely powerful. One of the four March sisters, Jo is a true tomboy, as Louisa May Alcott defined herself, and also an aspiring writer who searches for, and finds among the branches of an apple tree, the ideal space to read and to peruse the wonderful book of her aspirations. "Shining hours" is how Jo describes the time she spends reading in her old apple tree.[10] In the 1950s, in the United States, anonymous photographs can be found of girls reading among the branches and helping each other to climb a tree, holding a book in their hands. Jo March's green spirit is contagious. One of her most fervent admirers was Katharine Hepburn, who in turn played the lead role in the most famous film version of the novel, shot in 1933 by George Cukor. Katharine was a tomboy, too; she also climbed trees in the garden of her home in Hartford, Connecticut, and just as Louisa May Alcott's mother was a feminist, so the mother of the future actress was a suffragette and supporter of contraception and responsible motherhood. Her daughter would often remember helping her distribute balloons printed with the words "women's votes." It is an important theme, the transition from mother to daughter in the delivery of their duties, including that of awareness and the fight to obtain and defend it. Voltairine de Cleyre—an American anarchist, writer, and feminist, daughter of Hector de Claire, a French socialist on the barricades of 1848, and Harriet Elizabeth Billings, a descendant of an antislavery family from the state of New York—was perfectly aware of this. Voltairine, whose name pays homage to the father of the Enlightenment, was a child prodigy: at four she read the newspaper by herself, at six she composed poems and built her desk by planting a board between the branches of the maple tree in front of the family house. When, at the age of twenty-four, in 1890, Voltairine de Cleyre held her famous lecture *Sex Slavery* in front of the audience of Philadelphia's Unity Congregation, she would remember this experience, this convergence of such special space and time, and above all she would remember that the education of little girls does not include this freedom. Voltairine wrote: "Look how your children grow up. Taught from their earliest infancy to curb their love natures—restrained at every turn! […] Little girls must not be tomboyish, must not go barefoot, must not climb trees, must not learn to swim, must not do anything they desire to do which Madame Grundy has decreed 'improper.'"[11] Growing up in nature, and certainly

Voltairine de Cleyre loved Henry David Thoreau, helps one to discover one's own nature. Growing up in nature because this is the best education, the most honest, the most complete. Voltairine added: "'[You said] women can't rough it like men.' Train any animal, or any plant, as you train your girls, and it won't be able to rough it either [...] These are the effects of your purity standard, your marriage law."[12] In order for marriage not to be "sex slavery" a new education is needed. Sarah Orne Jewett knew this well when she told of the sentimental education of Sylvia, the protagonist of the 1886 novel *A White Heron*, where this wild girl climbs a towering pine tree in the thick of the woods and from that dizzying height she discovers the nest of a heron, the coveted prey for a young hunter she is in love with. Yet, for the same love for freedom that the bird's flight evokes, Sylvia will not reveal the place where the heron and its companion are hiding. Beah E. Richards, author of the poem *Keep Climbing, Girls*, one of Michelle Obama's favorite readings, knew very well that the treetop ascent was a winning metaphor even in the fight for civil rights of the African-American community.[13] And when Pippi Longstocking, Astrid Lindgren's elective daughter, made her debut in 1945 by inviting her new neighbors, the very bourgeois Tom and Annika, to climb the big tree in the garden of Villa Villecolle and to slide back down inside its hollow trunk, it really seems like she knew Carl Gustav Jung's *The Philosophical Tree*, published in the same year. A difficult, long, and painful process, that of Jungian individuation, which invites us to discover the roots of psychic life and to go back up to the green of the leaves to recognize our inner tree, archetype of growth and energy, and thus find a path to personal flourishing, often new compared to what was established in the darkness of birth.

Of course, Simone de Beauvoir knew everything about this right to spring blossoming in every season. Due to maternal prohibition, as a child Simone was not allowed to climb trees. How inappropriate, again. But in 1949, at the age of forty-one, Simone De Beauvoir wrote *The Second Sex* and announced that a liberated woman was being born, a woman free not to imitate the male in order to emancipate herself, but capable of finding the principle of self-determination within herself. In the first part of the famous essay, entitled "Destiny," Simone de Beauvoir quotes Alfred Adler when the Austrian psychiatrist and psychoanalyst states that a little girl climbs trees to rise to the level of males: "When a girl climbs trees, it is, according to him, to be the equal of boys: he does not imagine that she likes to climb trees."[14] Pleasure and that's it, this equality in the right to pleasure would be enough to say many things. That overwhelming pleasure of discovering one's destiny would be enough, maybe on a tree, maybe in front of a camera that portrays us sitting among the branches, alone, in twos, in threes, fives, ten other women, daughters, mothers, friends, sisters, smiling, confident, curious, maybe even happy.

1-Amy Lowell, *A Dome of Many Coloured Glass* (Cambridge, MA: Houghton Mifflin Company, 1912), 132.

2-Louisa May Alcott, *Little Women* (New York: Penguin Books, 1989), 95.

3-Ingeborg Bachmann, *Diario di guerra* (Milan: Piccola Biblioteca Adelphi, 2011); original title: *Kriegstagebuch*, (Frankfurt: Suhrkamp Verlag, 2011).

4-Angela Carter, *The Magic Toyshop* (London: Virago Press, 2008).

5-Marion Milner, *Una vita tutta per sé* (Bergamo: Moretti & Vitali, 2013); original title: *A Life of One's Own* (London: Routledge, 2011).

6-Douglas Collins, *The Story of Kodak*, (New York: Harry N. Abrams, Inc., 1990), 258, quoted in *The Art of the American Snapshot 1888–1978*, (Princeton, NJ: Princeton University Press, 2007).

7-Thomas Walther, *Other Pictures* (Santa Fe, NM: Twin Palms Publishers, 2000).

8-Jochen Raiß, *Frauen auf Bäumen* (Berlin: Hatje Cantz, 2016).

9-Laura Leonelli, *Io non scendo. Donne che salgono sugli alberi e guardano lontano*; English version: *I won't come down: Women who climb trees and look into the distance* (Rome: Postcart, 2024).

10-Louisa May Alcott, *Little Women* (New York: Penguin Books, 1989), 95.

11-Voltairine de Cleyre, *Sex Slavery. A Lecture*, www.theanarchistlibrary.org.

12-Voltairine de Cleyre, *Sex Slavery*, lecture published in *Lucifer the Light-Bearer*, 1890.

13-Beah E. Richards, *Keep Climbing, Girls* (New York: Simon & Schuster Books for Young Readers, 2006).

14-Simone de Beauvoir, *The Second Sex* (New York: Vintage Books, 2009), 85.

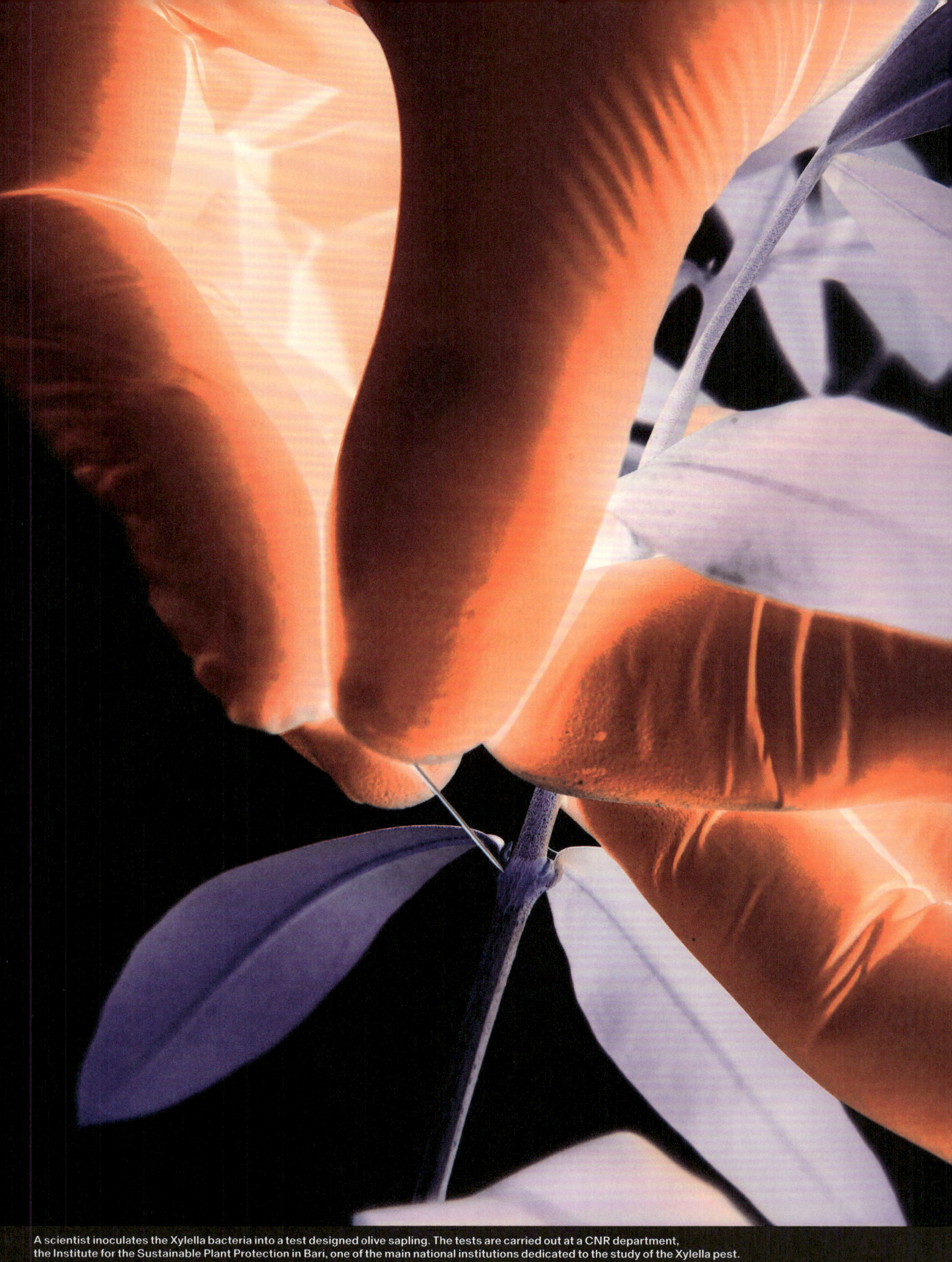

A scientist inoculates the Xylella bacteria into a test designed olive sapling. The tests are carried out at a CNR department, the Institute for the Sustainable Plant Protection in Bari, one of the main national institutions dedicated to the study of the Xylella pest.

Jean-Marc Caimi and Valentina Piccinni

THIS LAND IS MY LAND
A Photographic Journey Through the Xylella Epidemic in Puglia

Photographic duo Jean-Marc Caimi and Valentina Piccinni document one of the most serious plant epidemics of the past half-century, which has severely affected olive crops in southern Italy and now threatens the rest of Europe. This is their personal account from on-the-ground contact with farmers, agronomists, and scientists.

We have spent the last seven years documenting the impact of *Xylella fastidiosa*, a bacterial pathogen that has devastated olive groves in Salento, part of the Puglia region of Italy. Xylella causes Olive Quick Decline Syndrome, which rapidly kills olive trees and threatens the region's entire olive oil economy. Salento, once covered in olive trees, now has vast stretches of dry, dead groves, and farmers are struggling to cope with the loss of their livelihood. More than 40 percent of the region's olive groves are now affected by the epidemic.

Our project started in 2016, when the pest had just begun to take hold in the area around Gallipoli. What we saw was not just an environmental disaster, but the collapse of an entire cultural and economic system. The olive groves, the lifeblood of Puglia's economy and deep-rooted traditions, were dying. Farmers who had tended these trees for generations lost their livelihoods, their heritage and with them, their sense of identity. The rapid spread of the disease, exacerbated by climate change and the use of pesticides, added to the sense of helplessness, and many farmers had spent their savings on ineffective treatments.

In this climate of uncertainty and frustration, conspiracy theories quickly took hold. As the disease spread and olive trees withered, some farmers and locals began to question the official narrative. Theories circulated that the epidemic had been orchestrated by companies seeking to profit from the crisis. Others claimed that pollution or government corruption were to blame, and that the Mafia was involved. These suspicions were fueled by the slow response of the authorities and the seeming lack of progress in stopping the spread, creating a fertile ground for suspicion and speculation.

What struck us most as we followed the story was the human element that was often missing from the typical media coverage. News outlets tended to focus on economic statistics (how many hectares of olive trees were lost, the drop in olive oil production, the billions of euros in damages), but rarely did they delve into the emotional and anthropological toll. Behind the numbers were stories of grief, anger, and resilience. These considerations were among the elements that shaped our initial approach to the documentary project.

We took a more intimate approach. Using traditional black-and-white film and simple point-and-shoot cameras at first, we sought to capture these moments of raw emotion unobtrusively. One olive oil producer in particular opened his doors to us, allowing us to stay in his rural home and set up our darkroom in his mill premises—an act of solidarity. The tactile nature of analog photography was reflected the manual labor of the farmers. Working in these conditions, where dust, dirt, and heat clung to everything, infused our work with precious "real life elements," a value that we felt was essential to telling the story in its early stages.

  The local community welcomed us into their lives, and this human connection became the foundation of our work. It wasn't just about documenting the physical destruction of the olive trees, but understanding the emotional burden the farmers were carrying. We stayed in their homes, shared meals, and listened to stories of their deep connection to the land; some of the older farmers had even given personal names to their trees and were now watching them die one by one. Through photography, we aimed to provoke questions and emotions, prioritizing the people within the story over the object itself, the "who" over the "what," inviting the viewer into a reflective, thought-provoking process without offering simplistic or didactic answers.

  As our work progressed, it became clear that the scientific community was also an integral part of the story. The CNR (Centro Nazionale di Ricerca, or The National Research Council) in Bari became one of our key partners. We were given access to their laboratories to document their research into how and where the bacteria moved and spread geographically. We documented this side of the story using a variety of tools, including microphotography and digital color photography, to accurately record their work.

  In recent years, we have come into contact with the agronomists who are the link between modern science and centuries-old farming traditions. They are working with local farmers and peasants to identify wild olive seedlings that had somehow survived the epidemic. The idea was simple but revolutionary: these saplings could be naturally resistant to the bacterium, a result of cross-pollination and genetic adaptation. These young trees were taken to local experimental greenhouses, where they were rigorously tested for their resistance to the disease and their olive productivity. Agronomists grafted these seedlings onto more productive olive trees, such as the Leccino, in an attempt to create a new breed of Xylella-resistant trees. What made this approach so compelling was that it sought to preserve the local biodiversity of Puglia. Unlike globalized, lab-grown varieties such as FS17, which may resist the disease but have no connection to the land or its history, these new trees carried the heritage of the region. This delicate balance between tradition and innovation was central to the agronomists' work and to our understanding of the future of Puglian agriculture. We saw how the lives of the local people were intertwined, how the fate of the land was linked to both cultural heritage and scientific progress.

The six-year project culminated in a book titled *Fastidiosa*, released by the British publisher Overlapse. The volume reflects the multilayered nature of our work and serves as a testimony to this intense journey. The Xylella epidemic is more than an agricultural disaster; it's a story of human resilience, of the deep bond between people and their land, and a reminder of the importance of community and common roots in the face of adversity.

Salento has historically been characterized by an extensive monoculture of olive groves. Today the area demarcated as infected is nearly 8,000 square kilometers. That is 40 percent of Puglia's territory. A CNR (National Research Council) study predicts an alarming development scenario in the coming years in the absence of drastic action to form a buffer zone to prevent the spread. It was also estimated that the spread of the bacterium over the next fifty years could cost Greece, Italy, and Spain up to 17 billion euros.

In the first period of the spread of Xylella, farmers carried out drastic pruning of infected and yellowing branches in a vain attempt to stop the contagion.

Emanuele and Francesco Coppola (father and son) during the preparation of Kaolin treatment in Gemini (Ugento). Kaolin hinders the establishment and spread of insects, fungi, and bacteria and provides protection against high temperatures and water shortages.

    Kaolin could reduce symptoms caused by *Xylella fastidiosa* but there is no treatment to eliminate the virus. *Xylella fastidiosa* bacteria colonize the host plant's xylem vessels and block the water and nutrient flow with consequent desiccation of leaves and twigs.

A family of landowners in the early years of 1900. A "bad luck" person was cut out from the picture, probably imputed to a poor olive harvest year.

The insects belonging to the *Rhynchota* families like the Cicada (pictured) or the *Cercopoidea*, are believed to be the vectors of the disease of Xylella. They feed on contaminated xylem sap, contracting the bacteria, which is then transmitted to the next tree.

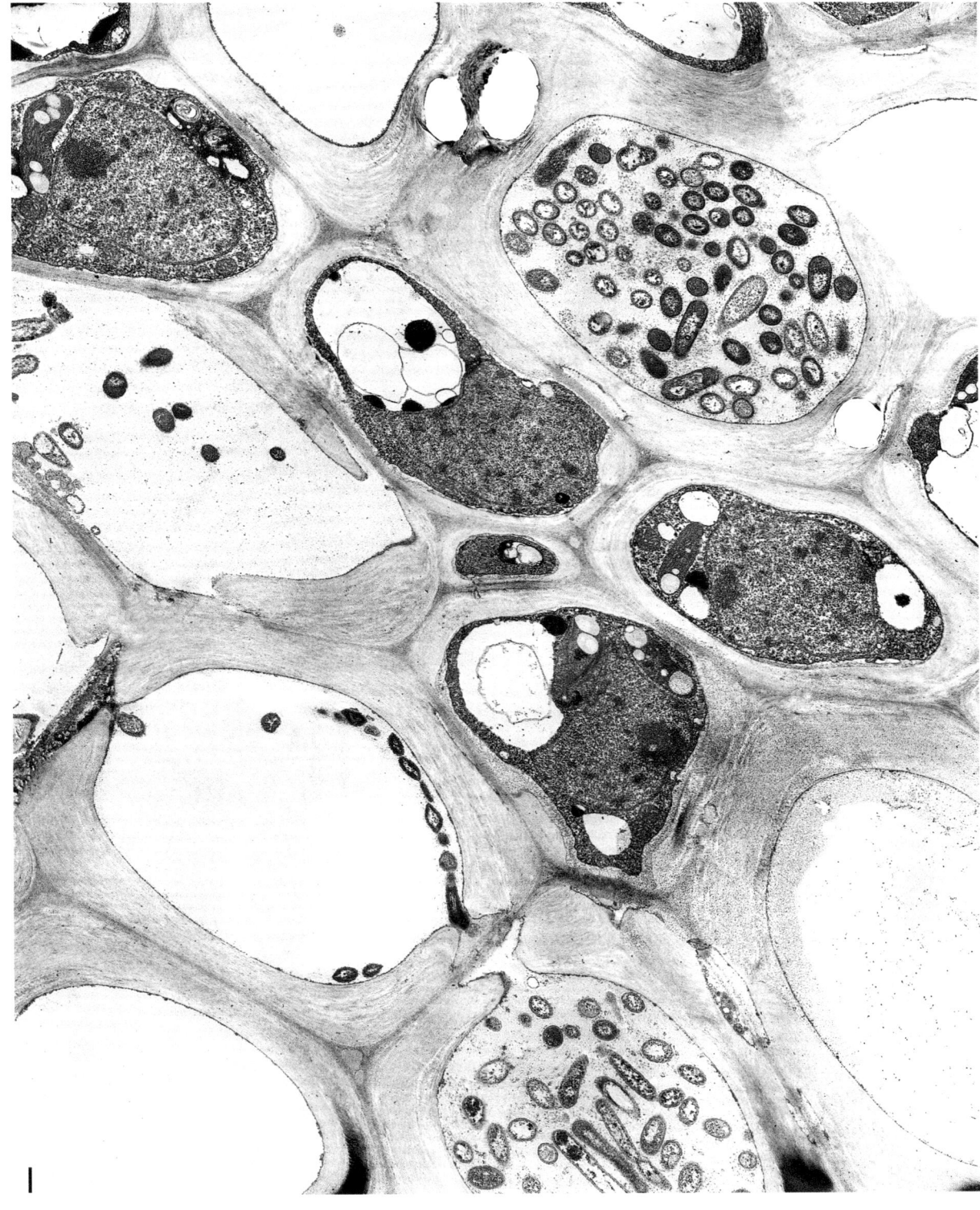

Xylella bacteria are clearly visible in the vascular tissue of an olive tree leaf. Their exponential growth blocks the xylematic vessels and causes the desiccation of the host tree.

Specially prepared shoots of spontaneous olive Xylella-resilient trees are grafted into multicentennial dying trees. This experiment, run by agronomist Giovanni Melcarne, is part of a larger project to find solutions to the Xylella pest. According to his theory, the Xylella bacteria is blocking the xylematic vessels of the branches but on a lesser extent the main tree body. Trees die by suffocation in absence of green leaves. By implanting Xylella-resilient new sprouts, there's a chance to save the whole tree.

Modern aerial remote-sensing techniques: hyper-spectral analysis and thermal sensor acquisitions allow an effective preventive identification of olive trees' desiccation.

A huge graffiti on a wall alongside the main road leading from Lecce, in the Salentine region, to Bari. The Xylella pest issue, which is causing an economic collapse of the entire Puglia region, is the perfect ground for conjectures. In the absence of a 100-percent confirmed official version, conspiracy theories flourish.
– "There is no epidemic of Xylella."
– "There is no scientific evidence to establish that *Xylella fastidiosa* is the cause of the olive tree desiccation."
– "Pollution of the ILVA steel factory in Taranto causes the groves' death."
– "Drones with herbicide sent by big companies like Monsanto are irrigating the fields during the night."
– "Monsanto will sell patented genetically modified, Xylella-resilient olive trees after the devastation is complete."
– "Trucks with herbicide sent by the real estate entrepreneurs irrigate the fields at nighttime. Space is needed to build resorts for tourists."
– "Scientists are corrupt. They earn a lot of money for useless experimentation for an invented pest."
– "Xylella is Mafia."

Xylella-infected trees are covered with nets to prevent the vector insect to escape and further spread of the outbreak. Ultimately, they will be cut down and removed.

A heap of wood logs of Xylella-infested groves. The contaminated trees are cut down to slow down the pest spreading and used as stove wood. Most of the sacrificed trees are multi-centennials.

Quotidian life in Nongriat

Morningstar Khongthaw and Wilfrid Middleton in Conversation with Kristina Pujkilović

THE STATE OF LIVING ROOT BRIDGES IN MEGHALAYA TODAY

Living root bridges are grown from the aerial roots of *Ficus elastica* by Khasi and Jaintia village communities in Meghalaya, India. They are an essential part of daily life: as a rural transport network, a key part of local culture and history, and a means of tourism income for several villages. The bridges also provide diverse ecosystem services, such as stabilizing slopes and preventing landslides. Moderated by Kristina Pujkilović, Wilfrid Middleton (Wilf) and Morningstar Khongthaw reflect on activism and tourism around the bridges, as well as the work of the Living Bridge Foundation, which Morningstar leads.

Kristina: Could you please introduce the living root bridges and your foundation?

Morningstar: I founded the Living Root Bridge Foundation in 2017, officially forming a group in 2018. We focus on the maintenance and conservation of living root bridges of the War Khasi sub-tribe of Meghalaya. We work with villages facing threats to these bridges and collaborate with elders and engineers who have built them for years. We involve local youth to pass down traditional knowledge. Over five to six years, we've made significant progress, including a partnership with the United Nations Development Program to support three villages responsible for around twenty-five bridges. This project has allowed us to document and preserve traditional knowledge that has been shared orally. Recently, I've become chairman of the heritage committee of the Khun Kur Longtrai Lai Kynthei (the landowner of the Raid Shabong, a community of fourteen villages) and begun to work with them on living root bridges. It's a significant achievement for our team.

Wilf: It's great to hear you describe your work, Morning. You've accomplished so much over the years. I've been part of some of these initiatives, and it's great to hear what you've achieved.

Kristina: Could you describe your personal background with the living root bridges, particularly your early experiences in the villages, and how these bridges have influenced your connection to your heritage?

Morningstar: I'd like to share a story from my childhood. When I was six, I had to cross a young living root bridge in my village with my father. I was scared and cried because it was connected by just a single root. My father, an experienced climber, encouraged me to trust the roots and guided me across.
In 2013 when officers visited my village Rangthylliang to film a documentary, I was living in Shillong. I returned to help translate for them, as they spoke only English. It was fascinating to see our village featured on television, showcasing its beauty. A friend pointed out that our living root bridges were something special. In 2014, I had my first encounter with a foreign visitor who wanted

to explore our village. I had to guide him despite my limited English, which was challenging but exciting. He stayed for five days, discovering the valley and its many bridges. That experience was significant for me, especially with the support of a local jungle guide named Pun.

Wilf: Can you share your thoughts on the significance of living root bridges in your culture and the steps you've taken to promote responsible tourism around them?

Morningstar: We recognized the urgent need to act regarding our living root bridges. When I asked a visitor why he was interested in them, he noted their uniqueness and cultural significance, emphasizing that increased tourism could benefit our village.

This insight led to the formation of the Rangthylliang Eco-Tourism Cooperative Society, where we explored ways to develop tourism sustainably. I visited other villages, like Nohwet, to learn from their experiences in promoting their bridges as tourist attractions. While the influx of visitors has brought positive changes, such as increased revenue and happier locals, it has also raised concerns. The village chief pointed out that the bridges were becoming weakened due to heavy foot traffic, prompting us to consider how to promote our site responsibly without damaging these unique structures.

Upon returning to my village, I organized a meeting with society members to discuss our findings and ensure that tourism would not harm the environment or the bridges. Our goal is to foster a responsible tourism experience that allows people to appreciate our culture without causing harm. This led us to expand the Rangthylliang Society into the Living Bridge Foundation (LBF) and gave the LBF its mission.

Kristina: I would like to know more about how to responsibly manage such heritage without succumbing to mass tourism.

Wilf: As Morningstar highlighted, there's significant potential in tourism to generate income and foster appreciation for the bridges. People are inspired when they visit and feel connected to them. However, we must be cautious, as there are many ways to approach tourism. For instance, the Nohwet-Mawlynnong Bridge has a road leading directly to it, complete with a large parking area. This setup may prevent village residents from benefiting adequately from the tourism revenue, as visitors can come and go without engaging with the local economy.

Moreover, it's essential to understand and respect the way of life in these villages, as it is the foundation of the bridges and the diverse cultures surrounding them. The bridges in Morningstar's village differ greatly from those in Nohwet-Mawlynnong or Nongriat, reflecting unique cultural contexts.

Morningstar: One important lesson I've learned in Meghalaya is the distinction between selling a destination and selling an experience. For instance, charging a small fee to see a waterfall is simply selling a destination. In contrast, selling an experience involves a deeper engagement with what the area has to offer. The heritage committee members have encouraged me to promote our fourteen villages as official tourist sites. However, I believe we need to first consult with experts who can guide us and provide valuable insights. We must develop our own criteria and measures before formally declaring these sites open to tourism.

My vision is to create a community of travelers who truly appreciate the experience rather than just visiting for the sake of it. I want to build a network of friends who can share their stories and experiences, promoting the beauty of our culture through word of mouth.

Kristina: This tradition is ancient, and its origins are somewhat unclear, passed down through many generations. However, we find ourselves at a turning point. With rapid urbanization, many young people are moving to cities, raising concerns about the connection of younger generations to these bridges. Are there enough young individuals in your community who are committed to maintaining the bridges?

Morningstar: In my village, I've observed a positive shift: young boys who once spent their time fishing are now discussing how to repair and maintain the bridges and plant the necessary Ficus trees. This changing trend is evident as the youth from Rangthylliang, Mawkyrnot, and Mynring villages take responsibility for adopting specific bridges in their communities, working to restore them.

On October 5, 2024, we officially appointed ten young individuals, chosen for their experience working with their parents in the jungle and using the bridges, especially during the monsoon season. They are eager to learn new skills and techniques for preservation. To encourage them, we plan to recognize their contributions annually through a ceremony organized by the heritage committee.

Wilf: In some places, the history of the bridges is very well understood, like in Nohwet-Mawlynnong, where they can pinpoint that a particular bridge is almost 200 years old. In other villages, the stories are less precise; someone might say, "It was planted by my grandfather," without knowing the exact timeline.

We took a step back to categorize these bridges based on their historical context: whether they were planted by someone currently alive, if there are living people who remember the planter, or if they predate living memory. This framework allows us to compare the many bridges across the Khasi Hills, though it doesn't capture the full richness of each site's history. Understanding these narratives and the passage of time is crucial for appreciating the bridges' significance. Claiming a bridge can be built in "ten to fifteen years" oversimplifies the reality. These structures require ongoing maintenance and a deep understanding of their purpose and history, which goes far beyond mere age.

Kristina: Growing the bridges takes years, and this perspective contrasts sharply with architecture and construction in Germany, where we often consider a lifespan of just fifty years before structures are replaced. The timeline for the bridges is entirely different. Morningstar, does this concept of time influence your daily life? Can you speak about how it affects others in your community? You are preserving something so old, precious, and unique, which surely shapes your experiences and values.

Shiningstar Khongthaw, a member of the Living Root Bridge Foundation.

Detail of a healing wound on one of the bridges.

Morningstar: This is a complex topic. Over the last ten years, discussions and research about the bridges have largely relied on oral histories from our elders. Time plays a crucial role in the growth and maintenance of these structures. For instance, I learned something new this year: during April and May, we focus on caring for the roots. Some roots grow from the previous year, while others emerge freshly in April, May, and June. The new roots are fragile and soft, requiring careful attention for a few months. Just last week, I realized how important it is to weave the soft roots properly, which is a lesson we learn through experience. Our dedication and belief in the timing of these roots are essential. This journey of learning is significant; we recognize that while there may be facts, there can also be exaggerated stories. We aim to convey the truth accurately, especially to the younger generation.

Kristina: How have you experienced changes in the environment and biodiversity of the bridges over your lifetime, and what insights have elders shared about these transformations? In the context of the climate crisis, what significant challenges do you see arising from these changes?

Morningstar: It's crucial to learn from the history passed down by our elders. Previously, we had eight months of rain; now it's only five or six, but the rain is more intense over that time, making it harder to dry clothes and impacting agriculture. In the past, people grew a variety of crops like oranges, potatoes, and jackfruit. Now, less than 10 percent of the valley is dedicated to orange farming, while around 20 percent is for vegetables.

Broom cultivation has surged in the last thirty years, which has decreased vegetation and soil fertility. We've seen more root bridges than a decade ago, but in 2022, we lost four due to climate change and unpredictable weather, including early monsoons. The village assembly, the Dorbar, is responding by designating more forest land and emphasizing the protection of Ficus trees around the bridges.

Ficus trees are considered guardians of the village, housing spirits that protect the environment from landslides and storms. In 2024, we held a consecration ceremony for a sacred forest, and this year, we'll establish a Ficus sapling center to grow these trees in areas with declining forest cover. It's encouraging to see traditional art institutions getting involved and recognizing the importance of grassroots governance in driving meaningful change.

Wilf: It's essential to recognize how embedded these bridges are in traditional practices, particularly in agriculture. While climate change will undoubtedly impact crop availability, more immediate threats arise from broom grass cultivation and mining. Deforestation endangers both the bridges and traditional farming methods.

Kristina: Given that the villages are located on high plateaus and the farmland stretches across the valleys below, could you share more about the historical development and geographical significance of these bridges?

Wilf: The Shillong Plateau features steep valleys descending toward the plains of Bangladesh. Villages are perched on the plateau while others sit in the valleys, often isolated from each other. For instance, two villages may be only two kilometers apart across a hillside, yet they can feel worlds apart due to limited contact. Traditionally, villagers would interact primarily at markets. Today, improved roads and communication have changed that dynamic, but historically, these isolated communities developed distinct cultural narratives. The bridges serve different functions depending on the village; in some, one person may solely use a bridge to access their land, perhaps inheriting the task from their family. In contrast, other villages may rely on a single bridge that serves the entire community. This diversity in usage reflects the varied stories and purposes behind the bridges.

Furthermore, across the different villages, each bridge tells a unique story. Some may fall out of use when the farmer who tended them is no longer around, as maintaining these living structures requires active care. This history is woven into each bridge, highlighting the diverse roles they play within their communities. Understanding this diversity is crucial to appreciating how these bridges integrate into village life and the broader landscape.
Even in one village, like Rangthylliang, one can find quite a lot of bridges ...

Morningstar: Between twenty-two and twenty-four.

Wilf: And each has its own story, size, shape, and function. While we can categorize them by age or use, their uniqueness remains. At the Professorship for Green Technologies in Landscape Architecture, we've conducted extensive research with Morningstar and others, focusing on how to adapt this knowledge to urban architecture in various climates.

Morningstar: The living bridges were built at a time when people relied on them for travel between valleys and villages. In the past, before modern roads and highways, these structures were essential for survival, providing access to markets and farmland. Some bridges were constructed by individual farmers for their specific crops, while others were collaborative efforts connecting multiple villages. This reflects their historical significance. Today, we have impressive new bridges built—for example, with steel for vehicles—but these older structures were built for people and animals, fostering community connections.

Wilf: It doesn't require extensive daily effort, but consistent awareness and observation of the bridges' changes are vital. This approach demonstrates a viable way of engaging with architecture, emphasizing inclusion. It's not just about a single designer; it involves various community members.

It's heartening to see young people returning to their villages to connect with the bridges, as they feel a sense of attachment to these structures.

Morningstar: Yes, the concept of the living bridges is thriving again as communities reconnect with their roots. While challenges exist—such as increased distances to the bridges due to shifting settlements—there's a renewed appreciation for these structures. People recognize their value beyond mere functionality; they now see them as integral to their identity. With global interest growing, communities are eager to showcase their heritage, inviting broader participation. Previously, only local farmers constructed the bridges but now government entities, tourists, and residents all contribute to their maintenance and creation.

Moreover, educational initiatives are incorporating bridge knowledge into school curricula, inspiring younger generations. Experts from various fields are now welcome to collaborate with us, highlighting the importance of sharing knowledge across tribes and communities. This cooperation emphasizes the environmental benefits of living architecture, particularly in the context of climate change, making it a sustainable model for the future.

Kristina: Thank you both very much. I think that was a fantastic closing statement. Your insights truly highlight the importance of community engagement and sustainability in architecture.

Wilf Middleton crossing Nongriat Access Bridge during a research trip in 2019

Fig 1. A bamboo- and rattan short-term bridge over which Ficus elastica aerial roots will grow.

Wilfrid Middleton, Zijing Deng, Elahe Mahdavi, and Ferdinand Ludwig

DESIGN—BUILD—GROW MEGHALAYA
Combining Vernacular And Modern Knowledge Through Making a Living Root Pavilion

As regenerative design gains popularity, vernacular architecture is a source of inspiration for architects. In rural Meghalaya, living root bridges hold the keys to challenges in urban settings such as the state capital, Shillong. This project combined vernacular practices in living root architecture with modern design methods to realize a growing pavilion in Shillong. With a firm understanding of vernacular practice and an openness to new design ideas, designers can transfer rural approaches, including radically different attitudes to change, to modern urban contexts. This report is adapted from a paper of the same title and authors in *Dimensions: Journal of Architectural Knowledge*.[1]

INTRODUCTION

Vernacular architecture is a product of a complex system of conditions: ecology, climate, society, economy, and culture. As architects turn toward regenerative design and development—buildings that regenerate the social and ecological systems in which they are built—we may learn from environmentally embedded vernacular architecture.

In Meghalaya, living root bridges are a centuries-old rural transport network formed from the aerial roots of *Ficus elastica* trees. Many bridges are collaborative social projects, have cultural heritage value, are ecologically highly significant. Most bridge-growers begin with a temporary bamboo bridge that is both a short-term solution and a frame over which to guide the roots as they grow (Fig 1). In this architecture, the bridges embody the societal conditions under which they are grown: they do not survive without regular maintenance. The materials used are products of not only the climate-geographic conditions of Meghalaya but also the social conditions: the knowledge of how to grow and treat the materials, and their structural limits.

In this project, we transfer living root architecture from its rural settings to an urban context. Shillong, the capital city of Meghalaya in north-eastern India, is grappling with a range of problems resulting from rapid urbanization. This study asks how vernacular and modern knowledge can be combined to transfer living root architecture from very remote rainforest valleys to a green space of the North-Eastern Hill University (NEHU) campus in Shillong. This is explored through the medium of a master's studio for students in Germany and India collaborating with the Living Bridge Foundation (LBF), a network of living root architects from around Meghalaya.

APPROACH

In examining the studio, this study applies a new design method to living architecture. Research by design, or RbD, finds creative solutions to open-ended or loosely defined research questions by exploring trial and error. In this case, research findings feed directly back into the structure through the manipulation of future growth. The process has three phases: pre-design (establishing the problem space), design (a cycle of visioning and problem-solving), and post-design reflections.

This is an intercultural, interdisciplinary study including people with varied focuses: some have a more specific focus (experts), some a more broader and general knowledge (students). At first communication is mainly one-directional: experts teaching students. Contrastingly, multidirectional communication is used in the design phase: students present phased results to the experts and they receive suggestions to refine their results.

In the pre-design phase, park sites were considered for a pavilion and the team were brought up to speed on key topics. The design phase saw three groups of students developing ideas for the pavilion in rounds, sharing and filtering ideas, resulting in a concept. With this, the team generated variants using parametric design in CAD. The core challenge in generating proposals was to design a short-term functional structure that facilitates the long-term structure's growth. The next step was to design foundations, columns, facade, joint, flooring, and sapling planters by studying Meghalaya's traditional architecture. This meant creating prototypes

Fig 2   Example of a model made of iron wire that shows how a ficus tree grows over an obstacle.

at 1:10 then 1:1 for details (e.g., the planters) and proposing a growth and manipulation plan.

OUTCOMES

In pre-design, students modeled growth patterns of *Ficus elastica* by making steel wire models (Fig 2). They also found (online) the "air-layering" bonsai method to stimulate aerial root growth that mirrors the traditional technique used in Meghalaya and backed it up with an understanding of botanical literature. Site investigations included an assessment of Shillong's climate and site microclimates, and making 3D digital models. Combining these with logistical considerations, a site at NEHU campus was chosen.

Three principles drove the pavilion design. It should fit the locale—the campus environment and Meghalaya; it should restore connections to nature; and it should be multifunctional. The conceptual form of the pavilion comes from mountains and caves—the celebrated landscapes of Meghalaya. Two curvy lines compose two different spaces: the higher level represents the mountain while the ground level creates an enclosed cave space. Use makes a pavilion into a place of life and culture. The enclosed cave is conceived as a shelter from monsoon storms and a maze-like space to explore. The mountainous top has different levels to give the feeling of climbing, and to create a viewing platform where people can rest and look out over the lake.

Development of the concept into a structural form is shown in Fig 3. Essential to the build is using a minimal amount of materials, which are sourced locally. The core material is bamboo, specifically the local variants *rñai* and *siej*, with rattan-tied junctions. All bamboos were (as per the traditional Khasi method) smoke-treated before use, reducing the starch content on which termites feed. *Areca catechu* planks (a by-product of betel nut farming) are used for flooring. Through these three materials, the construction mirrors a typical living root bridge. For planters, sparsely woven meshes are formed of bamboo and filled with moss and earth. *Ficus elastica* saplings are planted in these, mimicking the air-layering technique.

The proposed design was a three-dimensional grid of vertical and horizontal bamboos, the connections between which perform two functions:

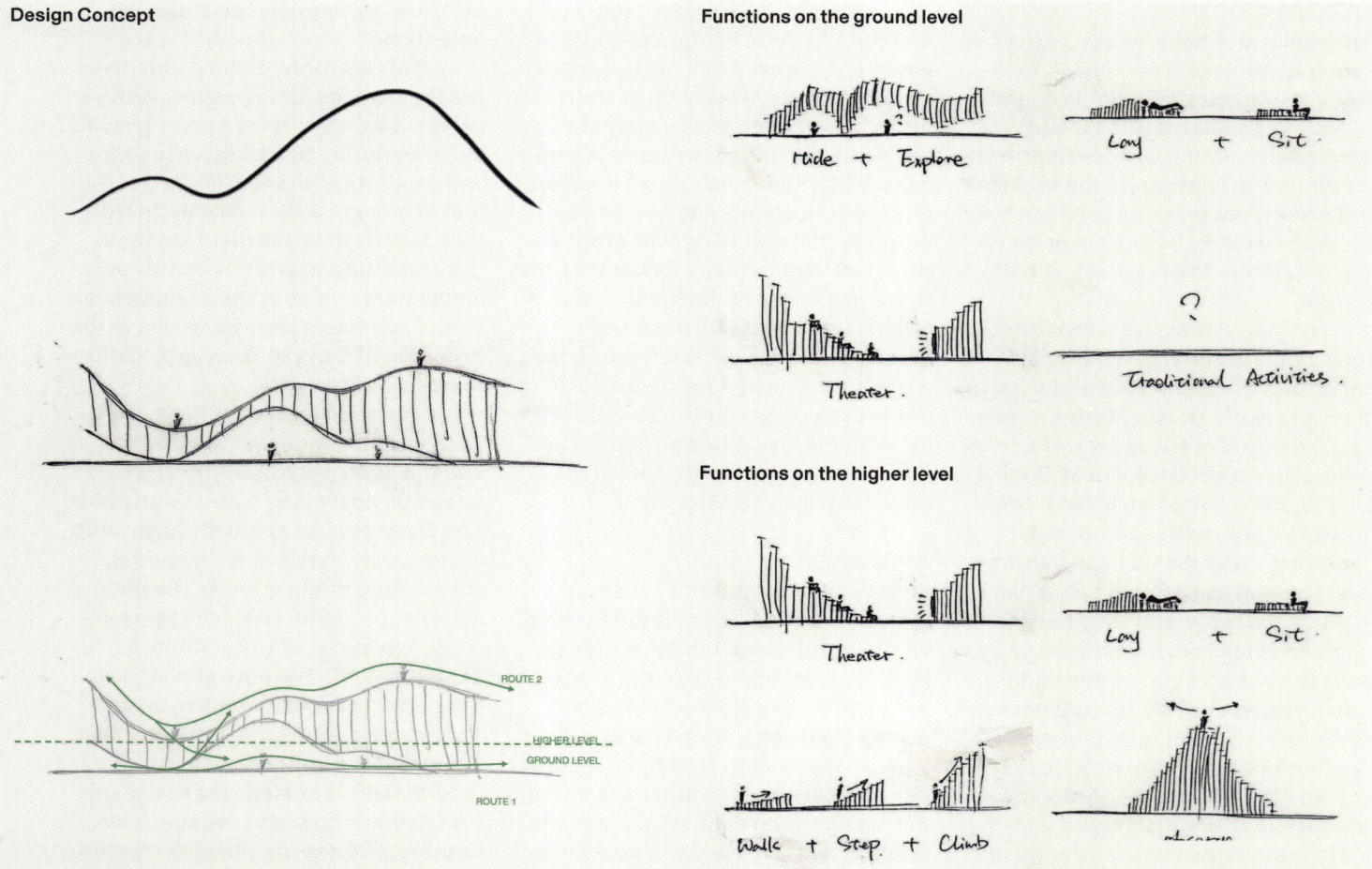

Fig 3   Progress of pavilion design to a structural form

Fig 4 Prototyping of the grid structure (top) and flooring system (bottom)

transferring forces across the structure and creating the shape, informed by parametric curves. Many points of connection ensure structural stability while enabling changes over time: replacing individual bamboos is made easy. This is essential as ongoing maintenance is a key part of living architecture.

A parametric model based on bamboo sizes and typical variability, grid density, site dimensions, and curved surfaces was built. This allowed considerations of buildability, such as ensuring the grid had gaps large enough for workers to reach through. The results are conceptual architecture forms with meaningful outputs: establishing the amounts and sizes of bamboo required and construction plans.

In addition to the grid, the design included pillars, flooring, and foundations. Columns that fit the grid were designed to allow scattered placement anywhere in the structure. The column also acts as a sapling planter by rising above the floor level. One-to-one prototypes helped the design team understand time taken for joint lashing (which became the most time-consuming practice in construction); the stability achieved with hand-tensioned rattan lashings; and the grid spacing needed to perform this handwork (Fig 4). The chosen foundation underpins parts of the four walls, with the bamboos sitting on padstones 60 centimeters belowground. The growth plan for *Ficus elastica* involves three stages (Fig 5). Planting (year 0), followed by guidance to the ground (up to year 5), and finally weaving the "cave" ceiling/"hill" floor (years 5–15).

Given the diversity of LBF members (from across Meghalaya) and their local building styles, some methods (lashing and bamboo cutting) were standardized and the design was simplified during construction. Following this, the pavilion consists of two halves: a stairway of many wide, short steps rising in one direction to the middle of the pavilion; and nine separate levels in a 3×3-grid at different heights in the lake-facing half of the pavilion. This reduced the number of lashed connections from around 4,000 to around 2,000.

The four walls were built precisely at first and used as guide points for the rest of the structure. The grown structure will begin to emerge over the coming years. Five saplings were

Fig 5 Growth plan for the saplings and aerial roots on columns

planted in December 2022. An unexpectedly dry spring in 2023 led to disappointing results—only one sapling grew significantly. Another set of saplings were planted in 2024, this time closer to the ground (Figs 6, 7).

REFLECTIONS
The project combined desk-based (lectures, research) and practical (sketching, modeling, prototypes) learning to gain a foundational knowledge of the properties of bamboo and rattan, and the growth properties of *Ficus elastica*. The potential interactions of vernacular and modern architectural methods are diverse. This study shows use of modern design methods (e.g., CAD & photogrammetry) that integrate vernacular knowledge (e.g., Ficus growth, considerations of annual maintenance) and techniques (bamboo construction and rattan lashing) to deal with challenges of an urban setting (e.g., complex supply chains and limited construction time). Part of the transition from rural-vernacular to modern-urban living architecture is considering the role of community participation in growth. In this regard, NEHU campus is a stepping-stone: a community of relatively like-minded people—university students and staff—and plans and rules for estate management and use. Periodic surveys are planned by NEHU students, capturing bamboo decay and root growth and planning interventions with the LBF. This urban design approach must be informed by the wider world of vernacular and modern design knowledge, which can both broaden the potential uses of vernacular architecture and give modern designers access to new fields of knowledge.

ACKNOWLEDGEMENTS
We would like to thank several parties for their help in this project. It was partially funded by The Ove Arup Foundation, a UK registered charity. The LBF and their members, particularly Shiningstar Khongthaw, were essential to the build. Thanks to staff at NEHU, especially Ibynta Tiewsoh. We are grateful to the participation of students from TUM and NEHU in the pavilion design and build, including Jasmin Raudensky, Zhiqing Zhou, Jennifer Ng, Thibault Bertin, Baiyu Chen, Ruike Sun, Viola Zhang, Meban Kharsiing, Harish Giri, Ibadianghun Wanniang, and Asif Rhizwan.

Fig 6   Sketches to show the gradual replacement of bamboo with Ficus trees after five, fifteen, and thirty years

Fig 7   Photo of the built bamboo pavilion in November 2022.

1–Please find the full version of this text, including all references and the list of all students and project partners in the original publication: Deng, Z., Ludwig, F., Mahdavi, E., & Middleton, W., "Design Build Grow Meghalaya. Combining Vernacular and Modern Knowledge," in *Dimensions. Journal of Architectural Knowledge*, 3(6) (2023): 127-150, https://doi.org/10.14361/dak-2023-0609

Telephone Booth, 1978. *Bird Cage*, 1978
Teepee Tree, 1978. *ZigZag Sycamore*, *Upside Down Tree*, 1978

Mark Primack

BOTANIC ARCHITECTURE
A Genealogy

Our Garden of Eden May Have Been a Roadside Attraction After All

I happened to come of age on the edge of an era, not sure if I was coming or going. I felt compelled to question everything I was expected to know, including my own choice of architecture as a profession. Fifty years later, on the occasion of this exhibition, I find myself once again on an edge.

    I paid for my education working as a union construction laborer; when I wasn't studying history, theory, or design, I was a beast of burden or a shovel. The first thing I understood about architecture was how very much it weighed. I carry that weight with me still.

    "Form follows function." "Less is more." "The plan is the generator." As a reluctant architecture student, I tested that third proposition, from Le Corbusier, by translating the floor plan of the Roman Baths of Caracalla into a topographic map. I maintained the same relationships of the spaces and their functions but defined them not by walls but by changes in elevation or foliage within a landscaped

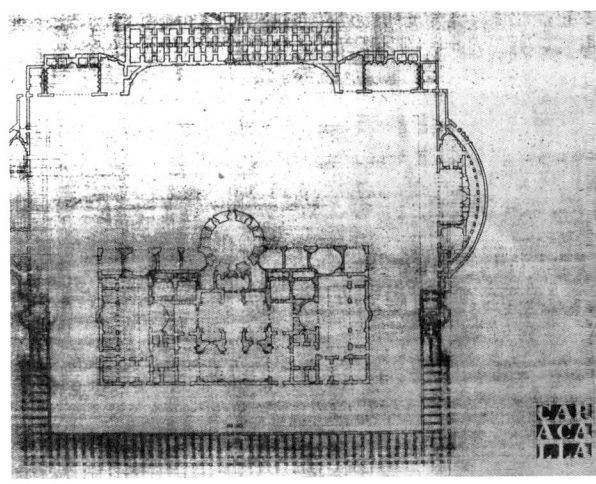

Fig 1   Caracalla plan

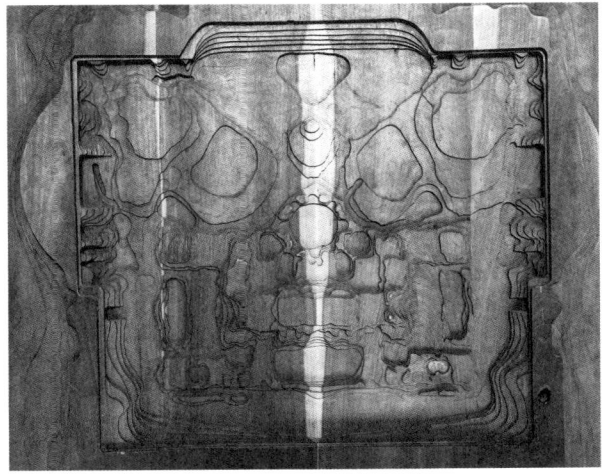

Fig 2   Caracalla model, 1972

garden under a Frei Otto pneumatic canopy. Services spread underground like roots. Pools became ponds; halls, plateaus; the building experienced as a garden (Figs 1, 2).

That project led me to London, to the Architectural Association. The task I set for my thesis there grew from a presumption that people were more alive in nature than in buildings. I wanted to define and perhaps prescribe the optimum environment for human habitation, and to imagine an uncompromised plan that might generate a less onerous future for a planet threatened by the fires of our material progress. I called it Botanic Architecture. This was 1973.

If natural evolution is a reactive adaptation to a changing environment, I imagined a proactive evolution, a willful return to the garden, and I mapped that out in my thesis. Ignorant then of Walter Benjamin, I fleshed out my thesis, like his *Arcades Project*, with quotes and references, letting others make my case while focusing on illuminating a path toward planetary wholeness with images meant to provoke or inspire. I searched for any and all examples of humans interacting or cooperating with nature to enhance or secure shelter. And I issued admonitions against technological shortcuts or compromises as I explored various regions of habitation (Figs 3, 4).

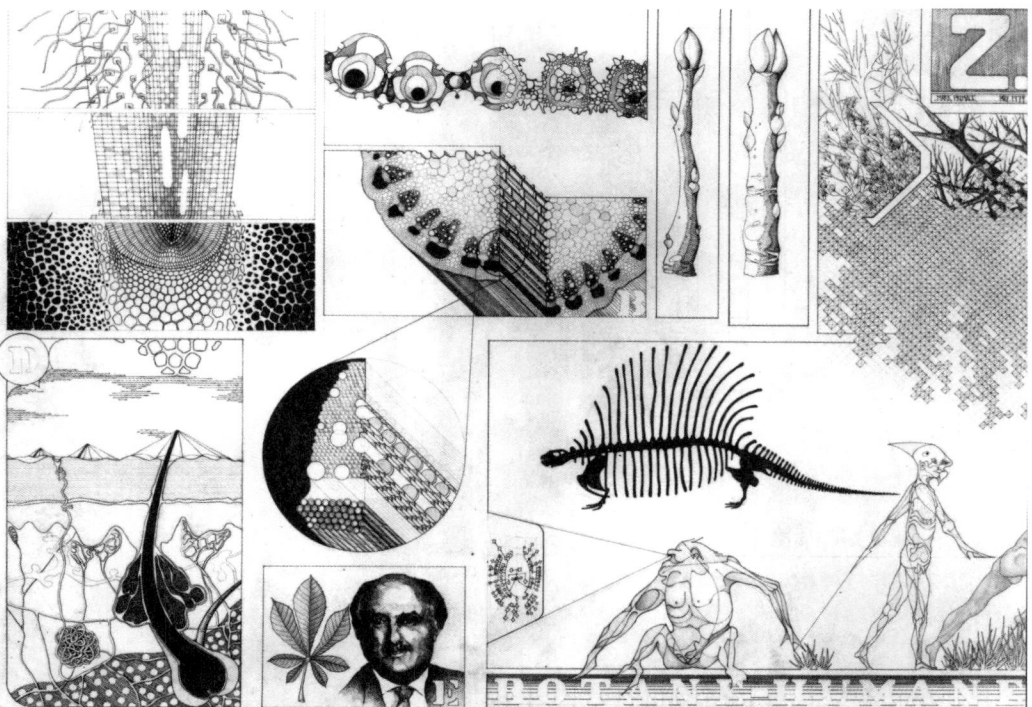

Fig 3   Botanic Architecture 3, 1974

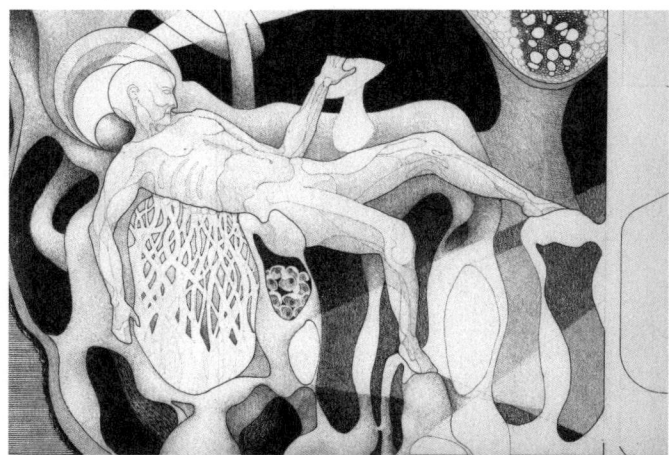

Fig 4   Botanic Architecture, Hibernation, 1974

There is very little of the agronomist in me. I am a scavenger, a forager. In gathering these odd quotes and precedents and building a case for a plant-based techne, I suggested that, as cities failed, London's green belt might become both a refuge and a learning field for Botanic Architecture—the declining city becoming a forest; the forest becoming a sanctuary, an intrinsic ecosystem inspired by poets, initiated by technocrats, cultivated by refugees, to be expanded and reinvigorated with each succeeding generation (Fig 5).

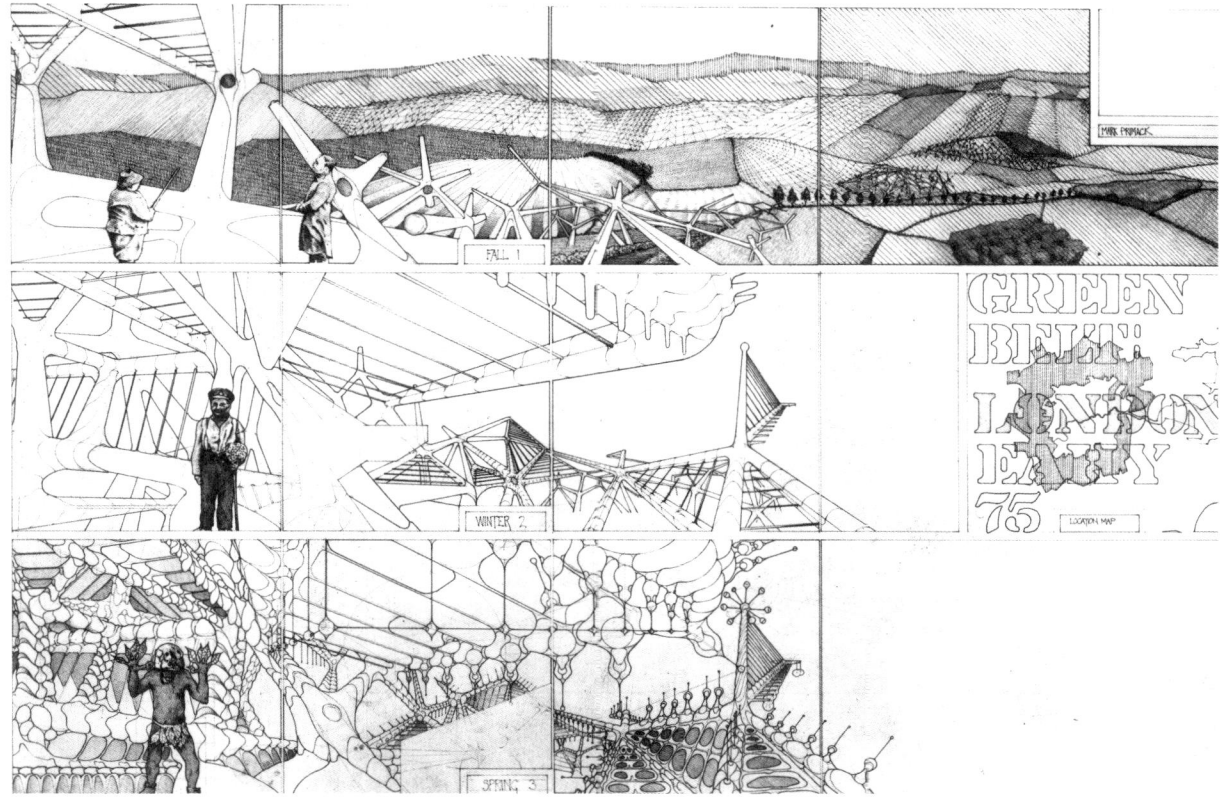

Fig 5   Green Belt 1, 1975

I can't remember why I left London for California in 1976. I don't surf. But once there, I discovered that ten dollars could secure a library card at the University of California in Santa Cruz, and then a publication called *CoEvolution Quarterly* agreed to publish an article on Botanic Architecture. So, I continued my research and wrote about wasps injecting growth hormones into leaf buds to generate galls, incubators for their own young. And about the Buddha's meditation beneath a serotonin-rich Bodhi tree (*Ficus religiosa*) as a coevolutionary phenomenon. And I speculated on further configurations of the Calcutta Banyan (*Ficus benghalensis*), a single tree cultivated—encouraged—to spread its shade over two hectares (Fig 6).

Fig 6   Calcutta Banyan

And then someone who had seen my work mentioned an abandoned roadside attraction ten kilometers away (and 10,000 kilometers from London) that I might find interesting, and I went and looked. What I found there was unique to this world but situated at the very heart of my thesis. All of it was about to disappear.

The creator of the *Tree Circus* was thirteen years dead at that point. The tourist spectacle he created had been sidelined by a highway diversion project. New owners had beggared attention by installing huge plastic dinosaurs in hopes of catching the eye of day-trippers bound for the beach. Prophetically, they'd changed the name to *Lost World*, and quickly failed to make a financial success of it. People no longer visited the trees. Locals were embarrassed by the dinosaurs. The property had been purchased by a developer; all would soon be long gone (Fig 7).

Fig 7   *Tree Circus,* 1978

It was left to me to perform a triaged documentation, with a borrowed camera and no resources. Drawing was the tool that allowed me to visually isolate the form of each specimen.

I was of course biased toward the architectural designs—the towers, spiral staircases, ladders, chairs, thrones, enclosures, arches, rood screens, etc.—but I had the sense to suppose that even the most playful designs might reveal technical feats of which I was woefully ignorant.

My second task was less time-sensitive but equally critical. I wanted to identify the person who had left behind these seventy-odd, unprecedented examples of horticultural virtuosity. And so, I became a de facto biographer. Axel Erlandson (1884–1964) was born into farming, but made of himself a naturalist, poet, musician, surveyor, draftsperson, mechanic, civil engineer, and orchardist, driven as much by inspiration and curiosity as by necessity. Beyond the fourth grade, school never got in the way of his education. What began as a simple observation of inosculation (self-grafting) among the trees in his nursery quickly grew from curiosity to experimentation to expression (Figs 8, 9).

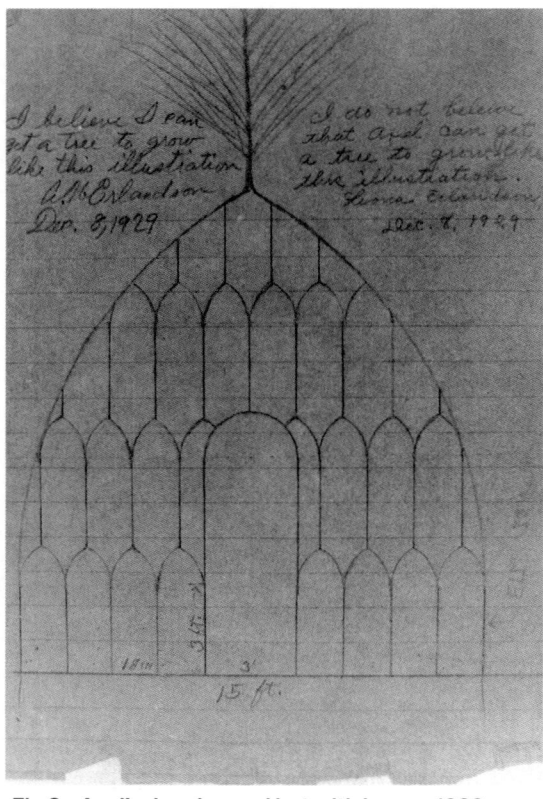

Fig 8   Axel's drawing and bet with Leona, 1929   Fig 9   Archway tree, c. 1932

As success followed success, and as Axel grew too old to work his farm, he devoted himself evermore deeply to his art. I wrote his story as much to inspire others as to fortify my own resolve. At the same time, I couldn't resist expanding Axel's experiments into more architectonic speculations, imagining his work going further than he had had the chance, the time, or the space to take it (Fig 10).

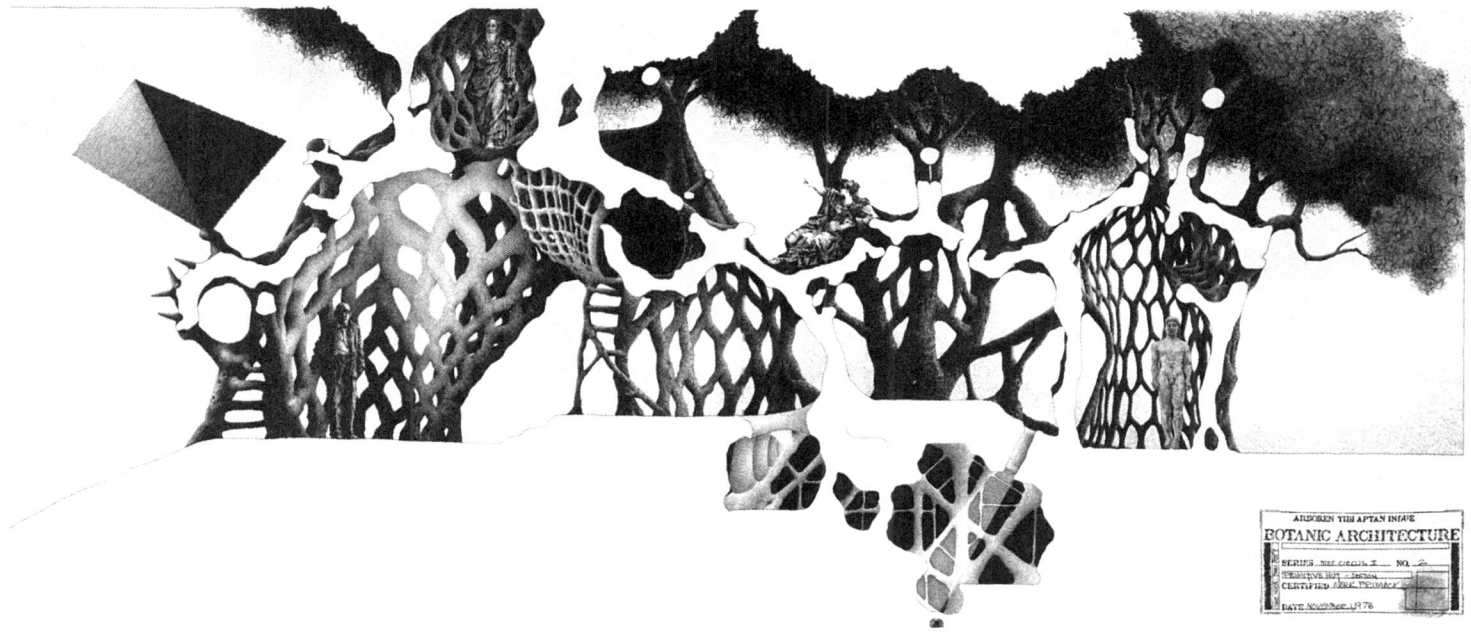

Fig 10 Botanic Architecture, Beaux-Arts section, 1978

I was still a stranger in these parts, without agency, but I made several attempts at spreading the gospel, pushing Axel's trees and my botanic ambitions through various design competition entries: Axel's chair in paradise for a furniture competition, his entire menagerie for a park in an alternate scenario for the redevelopment of Les Halles in Paris, and an imagined blockbuster biopic screenplay to launch tree pleaching as a media fad for a Japanese architectural futures contest.

When I thought I was done, I exhibited my *Tree Circus* drawings at a local gallery, which drew some attention within and beyond this community to the fact of the *Tree Circus* but also to its fate. Once the inevitability of its demise began to be questioned, I felt compelled to spend some years publicizing, politicizing, protesting, and trespassing (Fig 11)

Fig 11 Commando gardeners at *Tree Circus*, 1983

until finally twenty-eight of the surviving trees were purchased and moved to an amusement park fifty miles away (Figs 12, 13), in what

Fig 12 *Four-Legged Giant* at Gilroy Gardens

Fig 13 *Telephone Booth Tree* moved to the American Visionary Art Museum in Baltimore, Maryland

we today have learned to describe as a "happy ending." And when the site was emptied of live specimens, and at the insistence of David Nash, I rescued Axel's dead and decaying *Telephone Booth Tree* for display at a museum in Baltimore, Maryland, dedicated to "outsider," or "visionary," art.

With the departure of Axel's trees and left to my own devices, I ventured to propose the installation of a variation of Nash's Ash Dome in a traffic circle near the culmination of the very tourist route that had passed by the *Tree Circus*. Twelve sycamores (*Platanus sp.*) were to be planted, pleached, and pollarded at an elevation of five meters above current sea level.

But it would have been a public works project, and so the proposal went round and round and round the political process and never moved forward.

Here again, Axel Erlandson's story might be helpful. It was globalization's love child, tourism, that lent Axel's art its raison d'être in a postwar era that put a family car in every garage. And it was the free publicity of sensationalist publications like Ripley's *Believe-It-Or-Not* and *Life* magazine that brought in sightseers. Even then, it was Axel's daughter Wilma's job as a bank teller that paid the rent. But tourism and commercialism—capitalism—nonetheless gave Axel the agency to do his work. In 1946, he dug up and moved a dozen of his tree experiments the hundred miles from his failing farm to a parcel along a tourist route. By 1963, there were seventy-five healthy specimens there. But this is capitalism, and by the time I arrived in 1977, in the midst of a drought, eighteen had died. But again, this is capitalism, and so they're not all dead yet. In fact, the *Four-Legged Giant*, now at its third location, turned 100 this year.

Around the time I was born, Axel wrote:

> And if a person had a couple acres of good land (I have ¾ of an acre here) and forty or fifty years' time, then with the experience I have now (I learn more every year and have learned all this work by my own experimenting) I believe a person could grow a grove of trees of designs so much more intricate than I have here that they would make my present place look quite simple in comparison. But at my age (68 last December) it is of course useless for me to think of growing such a grove of trees when it takes such a long time.
>
> A number of people have asked me if there is anyone else who can take up this work when I lay it down: but I know of no one that could be trained to continue after me in this occupation.
>
> So, in a way it would appear that I have learned a kind of profession so late in life that I cannot carry it to near its ultimate possible attainment.
>
> But there may not be much lost if such is the case: because the principal things we need in this life are surely food, clothing and shelter, and growing these kinds of trees can hardly help to satisfy any of those needs. Perhaps it could be said about the growing of these trees as they called some activities during the first world war; activities which did not contribute in any way to the winning of the war were called "Non-essential industry."

By the time Axel's trees were ensconced in their latest roadside attraction, I had built an architectural practice, a home, and a family, and served on the city council in my adopted town.

Axel's trees and Botanic Architecture had become my "non-essential industry." My drawings, texts, documentations, and arcadian visions gradually receded to drawers and files until 2017, when Ferdinand Ludwig of *Baubotanik* wrote to me to ask if I would take him to see Axel's trees. And so here we are. But where exactly is that, in an era retroactively labeled the Anthropocene and in this next chapter of trees, and people, and habitation, and time?

Trees are shelter, arguably the first shelter and perhaps the most essential. Who hasn't taken refuge from sun, or wind, or rain, or chaos, beneath a tree? "Botanic Architecture" translates roughly to "Baubotanik," the consortium of talents unabashedly growing trees as architecture, as shelter. Of course, in the world I inhabit—career, art, academia—necessary distinctions are maintained and enforced between architecture and construction, between capitalized and vernacular art, between educated elites and the great unwashed. Axel understood and stayed in his place, without compromising his art. But those distinctions are marketing ploys. Instruments of exclusion. Detours. Roadblocks that no longer serve us.

My Caracalla Bath project was roughly contemporaneous with Archigram's "log and rock plugs." (It was in fact Archigram's founder and impresario, Peter Cook, who supported and promoted my thesis in London.) In both proposals, as in the original baths of Rome, a subterranean world of hidden high- and low-tech infrastructure offered a safe, climate-controlled nature to those who could afford access. But Botanic Architecture declared the medium the message. Nature would become all the infrastructure we needed, not through extraction but through adaptation.

"We shape our buildings and afterwards our buildings shape us," declared Winston Churchill from a devastated London in 1943. The premise of my London thesis and Green Belt initiative was equally simple: first we domesticate trees and afterward the trees domesticate us. It is a hope that reaches beyond profit.

The era upon whose edge I came of age was that of environmental awareness, when college students like me were first introduced to the basic concepts of "ecosystems." Ian McHarg's "Design with Nature" was still hot off the presses. In it, he recalled:

> Indeed, during the Depression there were many young men who would not submit to the indignity of the dole or it queues and who chose to live off the land, selling their strength where they could for food and poaching when they could not, sleeping in the bracken or a shepherd's bothy in good weather, living in hostels and public libraries in winter. They found independence, came to know the land and live from it, and sustained their spirit.

And Frantz Fanon had recently explained that capitalism is not infrastructure, it's superstructure. Its means are its ends. It had nowhere to go. Years before global warming and climate change, the Anthropocene, Capitalocene, precarity, and nomadism, postmodernism and humanism, decolonization and neo-colonialism had become commonplace tropes, one didn't need a weatherman to know which way the wind blew. Evolution appeared to be far more effective and enduring than revolution, and more promising by far than extinction.

So, I put a Botanic Architecture stamp on my *Tree Circus* drawings, with a provocation written in what its translator, Norman O. Brown, called "pig Latin": "If the tree fits, wear it." And that was that.

Simone Weil observed that a work of art has an author and yet, when it is perfect, it has something anonymous about it. Axel said it differently, though perhaps not as eloquently, from the other side. When asked where he got the notion to start it all in the first place, he responded, "One day, years ago, I suddenly got the idea. It seems that it was almost […] from some intelligence […] other than my own."

Fig 14 *Detourism Drawing, V.9 Tree Circus*, pencil drawing on card stock, 6" × 9", 2023

There are no primitive peoples, only primitive technologies. Again, Le Corbusier. On the face of it, nothing is more primitive than fossil fuel. We understand the problem now. Nature is anarchic and balanced; capitalism, ordered and entropic. There is no one right tool for the job. Einstein had something to say about solving a problem with the tools that created it. Our most powerful tool, language, has been failing us for some time now. Perhaps that is why I felt compelled to draw Erlandson's trees, and why I still draw before I write. Tactile subjectivity may still prove more deeply essential to human expression than language itself. It worked for Axel. When children asked him how he got his trees to grow that way, he told them he talked to them. Without ever moving his lips.

    Three years ago, I had reason to revisit the *Tree Circus*. The photo I translated into this melancholic drawing was taken when I was part of the story. The *Living Heart* tree had been toppled by a neighbor's tractor. We guerrilla gardeners had propped it upright with a winch, and I'd swaddled its sunburnt trunk in canvas. The garden hose I'd smuggled in lies restless like a snake beside the *Teepee* tree. But the *Lost World* shed, stucco-ed to resemble a cave and topped with a presumably Mesozoic bear, was gone. In its place I drew one of the "castles of vanity" from Hieronymus Bosch's *Garden of Earthly Delights*. Actually, five hundred years ago, Bosch named the piece *The Millennium*. Actually, "Bosch" was not his real name; "bosch" means "forest" (Fig 14).

    Now, and again, I return to Simone Weil to put the *Tree Circus,* Botanic Architecture, the work of *Baubotanik*, David Nash, and others here in context. Art for Weil was the symbol of the two noblest human efforts: to construct and to refrain from destruction. Good luck to us all.

Édouard François

MY ENGAGEMENT WITH GREEN ARCHITECTURE

I have been working for more than twenty-five years on the topic of architecture and nature, and I still haven't exhausted its possibilities. Here, I am sharing a few insights from my reflections, all of which are still relevant and have served as sources of inspiration for all of this time.

AT THE CORE OF MY WORK: CONTEXT

During my studies, context was a minor topic of discussion. Yet, I have made it the core of my approach. The constant theme in my work is not the plants themselves but rather the context, a setting that influences architecture. For this reason, I have never defined myself as a landscape architect.

I am very committed to the human scale, hence my interest in design. A simple door handle is an invitation for the human hand. When choosing between two solutions—one somewhat "dull" but valuable, and the other "beautiful and elegant"—I always choose the more functional one, even if it is less aesthetic. Over time, function always prevails.

EVOLVING TOWARDS URBANISM

I first worked outside cities, then gradually moved closer to the urban environment. As my reputation grew, I was able to build in cities, and today, I design cities. By integrating landscape and nature, I introduced an element of invisibility in my urban projects to escape the feeling of density. Rows of trees, perfectly trimmed into parallelepipeds, do not create the same impression of density as a row of buildings of the same size.

THE GREEN FAÇADE: A STEALTH SOLUTION

The Green Façade was my response to making urban density more acceptable. Cities must densify to combat urban sprawl, and the contextualized green façade helps to visually soften this density. Over time, greenery has taken on different forms to address various challenges, and I am far from having exhausted all its potential.

CONTEXT: A FOUNDING ELEMENT

My first projects were in the countryside, near forests. In Jupilles, near the Bercé forest, I designed a hamlet of cottages. Midway between forest and village, my constructions respect a status quo: they have become hybrids, half-forest, half-building. The forest advances towards the village, forming inhabited wooded masses, while the village breaks apart into wooded masses as it approaches the forest. The message is simple: we must stop encroaching on nature. It is time to pause and mend the edges of cities with the natural environment.

FRUGAL ARCHITECTURE

Doing less architecture and more in the landscape was an obvious solution. Such highly economical solutions anticipated the frugality that has now become essential. These "enlarged" or "enhanced" projects had to fit into their landscape in the broadest sense. I worked extensively on the wooded extensions of the buildings. Dentistry illustrates this approach well: today, we treat the gum as much as the tooth. If every building considered its neighbors, we would genuinely succeed in creating the "City."

Fig 2   *Jupilles:* The Bercé State Forest, in front of a guesthouse nestled within a grove of thuyas and pruned prunus trees shaped into topiary. Temporary fencing.

Fig 3   *Jupilles*: Summer view of the guesthouse façades surrounded by evergreen thuyas and deciduous prunus groves

EXTENDING PARKS INTO THE CITY

In an urban development plan by Christian de Portzamparc, I wanted to extend the central park by lining its edges with green buildings, thus creating a vertical extension of the park, like a cyclorama in a television studio. The park is thereby amplified, gaining in depth. Named Tower Flower and adorned with 400 pots of giant bamboo, the building was designed as an extension of this park.

ENGAGING ALL THE SENSES

Working with nature always brings unexpected occurrences, which I call "collateral benefits." In Paris, at Porte d'Asnières, the Tower Flower building began to rustle in the wind. Residents told me they slept better thanks to the rustling of the foliage, which created a sense of grandeur. The humus enriched the experience by stimulating the sense of smell.

NEW USES: LIVING IN TREES

For my project *L'Immeuble qui pousse* ("The Growing Building") in Montpellier, I planted large trees very close to the façades. Then, I designed actual treehouses within these trees, accessible from the living rooms of the apartments via footbridges. This redefines and blurs the indoor and outdoor boundary while offering new uses. These extensions are like balconies suspended in the tree canopy. The commercial success was immediate.

THE POROUS FAÇADES

To complement the trees, I designed the building's envelope as a porous biotope, ready to be colonized by nature. We integrated an automatic irrigation system into this stone façade, made of gabions. As the interstices became damp, they began to host microorganisms: first algae, then lichens, grasses, shrubs, and eventually trees, which were able to thrive in the fertile humus.

This was my first green façade, consisting of several layers of stones held in place by stainless steel mesh. Highly porous, it became an actual living wall. In summer, irrigation keeps the façades cool, and none of the residents need air conditioning, despite it being common in the region. Another "collateral benefit" is its ability to absorb noise; it provides excellent sound insulation. This contributes to the city's "sound invisibility," offering a surprising urban experience.

THE CONTINUITY OF MYCELIUM

Bit by bit, I became interested in the continuity of the fungus mycelium to create "highways of life." I stopped thinking of nature in terms of isolated pots and began to imagine it as a continuous, unbroken network: the continuity of mycelium. Continuity is more important for living organisms than the amount of soil itself. I realized how much we, as architects, fragment living ecosystems. So, I created these "highways of life" at the foot of my buildings. Today, I take great care to foster this continuity; my pathways act like bridges, allowing life to flow underneath.

BACK TO THE SOIL

My shift towards in-ground planting began a few years ago. If we planted greenery on façades starting from the ground, we would gain efficiency and ease of maintenance. The challenge, however, was the demand for immediacy—clients often wanted instant results. In Nice, for the Le Ray project, I planted climbing plants in the ground and others in pots placed higher up on the façades. Working from the assumption that the upper growth limit of climbing plants is unknown, I grafted all the plants together, making them a single botanical entity. To ensure the sap from the mother plant in the ground could nourish those planted higher up, I connected all the pots to the earth to guarantee a consistent piezoelectric effect.

After three years, I turned off the automatic irrigation for the pots on the façade, and all the vegetation began relying solely on the mother plants below. On both the north and south façades, the plants fused into a single, multi-stemmed organism in the botanical sense. This technique is known as anastomosis.

Two young German architects, Ferdinand Ludwig and Daniel Schönle, are working on plant anastomosis as a construction system. They envisioned an elevated walkway supported by a temporary, removable structure. Once the tree grafts take hold, the structure is dismantled, and the trees themselves then support the walkway.

URBAN AGRICULTURE

More recently, I have turned my attention to edible landscapes, or "foodscapes," initiating my work on urban agriculture. I applied this concept in the ZAC du Parc d'Affaires, where over three hectares of rooftop space were vegetated. This ensemble forms a sort of farm spread across approximately twenty buildings, connected by walkways to facilitate maintenance. Some rooftops house ponds for insects, others have greenhouses, composting areas, and production fields. The entire operation is managed by an Association Syndicale Libre (ASL), an organization that oversees the shared interests of the property owners. The ZAC du Parc d'Affaires is the largest urban agriculture zone in France, where each co-owner holds a plot as well as a share of its produce.

COMBATING URBAN HEAT ISLANDS

As cities are becoming warmer, urban heat islands are forming. I have noticed that plants play a crucial role in counteracting these heat islands. The evapotranspiration of foliage cools the air and lowers perceived temperatures.

In Bordeaux, at the heart of the UNESCO World Heritage site, we created new avenues that serve as urban parks, providing access to housing, hotels, and shops. The issue of heavy delivery vehicles prompted us to rethink the soil composition, transforming it into vegetated roadways. Trees were planted in the aerodynamic turbulence zone to maximize the evaporative effect in the wind. The seemingly random placement of trees, as found in a forest, contrasts with the rigid alignments of trees commonly found in cities. In this new urbanism, every available space has been repurposed for plants. Between each adjacent building, climbing plants form green separators that, from a distance, appear continuous.

ORNAMENTATION

Our current project involves a historic building on Rue aux Ours in Paris. Built in 1907, it was the first Art Nouveau building in the city. Unfortunately, its history took a turn for the worse in 1981 when the new owners stripped the building of its ornamentation. The beautifully sculpted foliage by artists Bédard & Suau was sanded away. In response to this destruction, I wanted to restore the building's former grandeur. Living trees will replace the lost ornamentation. Planted in the stone walls of the façade, these trees will restore a vegetal aspect to the building. We will place pots inside the building, on the opposite side of the façade, with 10-centimeter openings to allow the trees to flourish outside, ventilated and irrigated. This way, the restored foliage will cool the historic south-facing façade.

To recreate the lost Art Nouveau interior decorations, we turned to artificial intelligence to generate Art Nouveau aquatic plant motifs. These designs were entrusted to Bourdeau, a company renowned for its expertise in heritage restoration, to reinterpret them in plaster bas-relief.

I DIDN'T ONLY BUILD WITH NATURE

Around 2006, vertical gardens were all the rage and everyone rushed to win bids. These were façades without soul or meaning, built indiscriminately, often with no thought for irrigation or maintenance. Cities even changed their urban planning regulations to mandate plants on façades, sometimes drawing inspiration from my projects.

At that point, I decided to end my "green period." For the luxury hotel Le Fouquet's Barrière, I designed a Haussman-style façade "walled off" in architectural concrete, randomly pierced with identical windows to light the interior suites. In a Haussmannian context, you can't outdo a Haussmann building … it's like a ceramic tooth meticulously aged to match the imperfections of its neighbors!

Context was still at the heart of my project. I only returned to greening later, focusing on planting directly in the ground. With climate change, I can no longer do without it; there's also the issue of biodiversity, not to mention that hardscapes have become increasingly unappealing.

A DEEP KNOWLEDGE OF PLANTS

I believe I have a good understanding of plants and the plant kingdom. Today, I can pass on this knowledge in two simple sentences:
1. Nature is so complex that no one can fully grasp it in a lifetime.
2. If nature is so complex that no one can fully grasp it, then invent nature—because it exists.

In practice, I define the type of plant, and ask botanists to search for them. For example, for a kindergarten I designed in Thiais, I envisioned a floating green copper volume, cantilevered at 25 meters into the trees, with twisted branches around the building. I wanted trees with large, heart-shaped leaves and stemmed blooms so that the children could admire the flowers in spring. The botanists brought me *Paulownia imperialis*, which was even more beautiful than I had imagined.

People sometimes think I have universal knowledge of plants—I just know those two sentences.

Fig 4 Modell Montpellier, The Growing Building

Fig 5 Tower Flower Model: White concrete and grey concrete, white marabou feathers

Fig 6   Montpellier: The Growing Building: Façades with planted gabions, a treehouse in the plane trees, cold paint, and a ground-level grove of laurels

Fig 7   Nantes Water Treatment Model: Dried plants, plaster, slate, resin, and twigs

Fig 8   Buffon School: A 25-meter cantilevered structure amid paulownias, with a copper and frosted glass façade, PVC elements, and a steel framework with irregular braces

Fig 1   Jami, *Alexander the Great in a Tree Pavilion*, folio from *Haft Awrang* (*Seven Thrones*), 1610–1620, India, watercolor and gold on paper, Aga Khan Museum, Toronto.

Roberta Martufi

LIVING IN TREES?
A THOUSAND-YEAR HISTORY

Building a tree house is a dream that few may have the chance to realize, and perhaps even fewer would be brave enough to live in a tree, like Baron Cosimo Piovasco di Rondò, described by Italo Calvino in the *Baron in the Trees*.[1]

In the contemporary world, tree houses are usually associated with that carefree period of life that is youth; however, in the thousand-year history of building, they have had a very different origin and use.[2] The first tree house that we know of was built by Emperor Caligula (AD 12–41) in his villa in Velletri. Pliny the Elder describes it as a large dining room in which the emperor, comfortably reclining on the triclinia, could host up to fifteen guests accompanied by their servants.[3] Built with a wooden platform supported by the branches of a large plane tree, it was a sort of large nest where he could take refuge, rest, and receive his friends. Pliny describes another tree house, that of the consul Licinius Muscianus in distant Lycia, which was more of a house inside a tree than a tree house. A cave-like space of about 81 feet was dug inside the trunk where the consul could entertain up to eighteen guests, sheltered from the wind and rain.[4] In ancient times, multiple types of tree houses were built, each one interacting with the tree structure in a different way. The presence of water in these structures, both for games and for food is well documented, revealing how refined Roman forestry, engineering, hydraulic, and topiary techniques were. The houses described by Pliny can in fact be considered an extreme application of topiary and an extension of the villa into the park (Fig 1).

With the collapse of the Roman Empire, the villas and even more so, the parks, were abandoned. Life withdrew within castle walls; however, at the same time, the religious hermitage took hold. The first Christian monks often lived in "hermitages," often natural caves or humble dwellings in isolated woods and deserts. Tree houses, originally linked to the nobility's "sweet idleness" (*dolce far niente*), had completely changed character, then built as religious refuges in the forests.

Among the saints and the dendrites—as they were called in the East—Saint Anthony of Padua and Saint David of Thessaloniki (Fig 2) are the saints most often depicted among trees. In particular from the hagiography of Saint Anthony we learn that, in the last years of his life, he had a sort of cell built on a large walnut tree in the woods surrounding the hermitage (Fig 3). Many artists, including Vitale da Bologna, (Fig 4) and Hieronymus Bosch,[5] show him studying, writing, or performing miracles in his "green hermitage."

The first written manual on tree-house building, in the *Ruralium Commodorum libri XII* by Pietro de Crescenzi (1233–1320),[6] illustrates the techniques in detail. In a chapter entitled "Of the gardens of the kings and other rich lords" (De Giardini de Re & degli altri ricchi Signori), he recommends taking up the tradition handed down by Pliny; the gardens should have "a palace with fireplaces and rooms made only of trees in which the King or Queen can live with their barons or ladies in dry and clear weather."[7] According to De Crescenzi, the most suitable trees were willows, poplars, and olive trees, which thanks to "poles and perches and ties" could grow straight up to 10 feet from the ground.

It was with the Renaissance that classical models were rediscovered, and attempts were made to emulate the ancient splendor, to experience the "pleasure of living in a villa" and build tree houses in the parks. Among the works that describe how the Renaissance man imagined his dream garden, the *Hypnerotomachia Poliphili* by Francesco Colonna,[8] printed in Venice in 1469, gives a detailed description of a house that matches De Crescenzi's description, written almost two centuries earlier. The text, enriched with precious engravings, helps us imagine a real house built with cypresses, cedars, lemons, oranges, etc., with a door and windows, and all the most typical elements of a building. The structure described in the *Poliphili* was divided into two levels where the ceiling was made of thick intertwined branches, fragrant thanks to the presence of flowers and citrus fruits.

The *Hypnerotomachia Poliphili* spread rapidly through the main courts of the Italian Renaissance and was an inspiration for the gardens of the nobility's villas. The presence of large trees on which these structures were built is documented both by iconographic images and written texts. In the lunette of the Medici villa of Pratolino painted by Giusto Utens, (Fig 5) and in the engraving by Stefano della Bella (Fig 6) of the same villa, a spiral staircase embraces the trunk of a large oak. The writings of Giorgio Vasari[9] and Michel de Montaigne both mention a comfortable staircase to "a small pavilion among the branches of an evergreen tree, but much thicker than all those encountered up to now,"[10] located in the park of the other Medici villa of Castello.

Many agricultural treatises demonstrate how this was a widespread practice. For instance, Agostino Del Riccio writes "there was a wood with all the appearances of a house made with the artificial hand of a master. Where there was a hall, a bedroom, a kitchen, a pantry, and rooms, all these rooms were covered with greenery and various branches from different plants. In addition, you will see a small table in the hall in the middle from which comes crystal clear water both for drinking and for bathing the guests after the banquet for amusement and pranks."[11]

Other significant Renaissance gardens include those of Schaffhausen and Baden described by both Fynes Morrison and Michel de Montaigne. The Schaffhausen structure impressed both authors for its size "twenty paces in diameter"[12] and because "… where also is a Lynden or Teyle tree, giving so large a shade, as upon the top it hath a kinde of chamber, boarded on the A chamber in floore, with windowes on the sides, and a cocke, which 'Linden being turned, water fals into a vessel through divers pipes, by which it is conveyed thither for washing of glasses and other uses: and heere the Citizens use to drinke and feast together, there being six tables for that purpose.'"[13] Montaigne explains in detail the technique used to create the floor, walls, and the roof of the circular loggia with branches.[14] Seventeenth-century engraver Matthäus Merian's representation of the square of Altötting (Fig 7) documents that these structures were also built in public spaces; in Basel (and likely it was the same in Baden and Schaffhausen) assemblies were held under the trees. These were the focal point of German life from the end of the

Fig 2 Anonymous, *Saints Simeon Stylites the Elder and David of Thessalonica*, fifteenth century, Monastery of Vatopedi, Mount Athos

Fig 3 Anonymous, *Saint Anthony in a Walnut Tree*, c. sixteenth century, formerly the Robert Forrer Collection

Fig 4 Vitale da Bologna, *Tales of Saint Anthony the Abbot*, c. 1340, tempera on wood, Pinacoteca Nazionale di Bologna, inv. no. 563

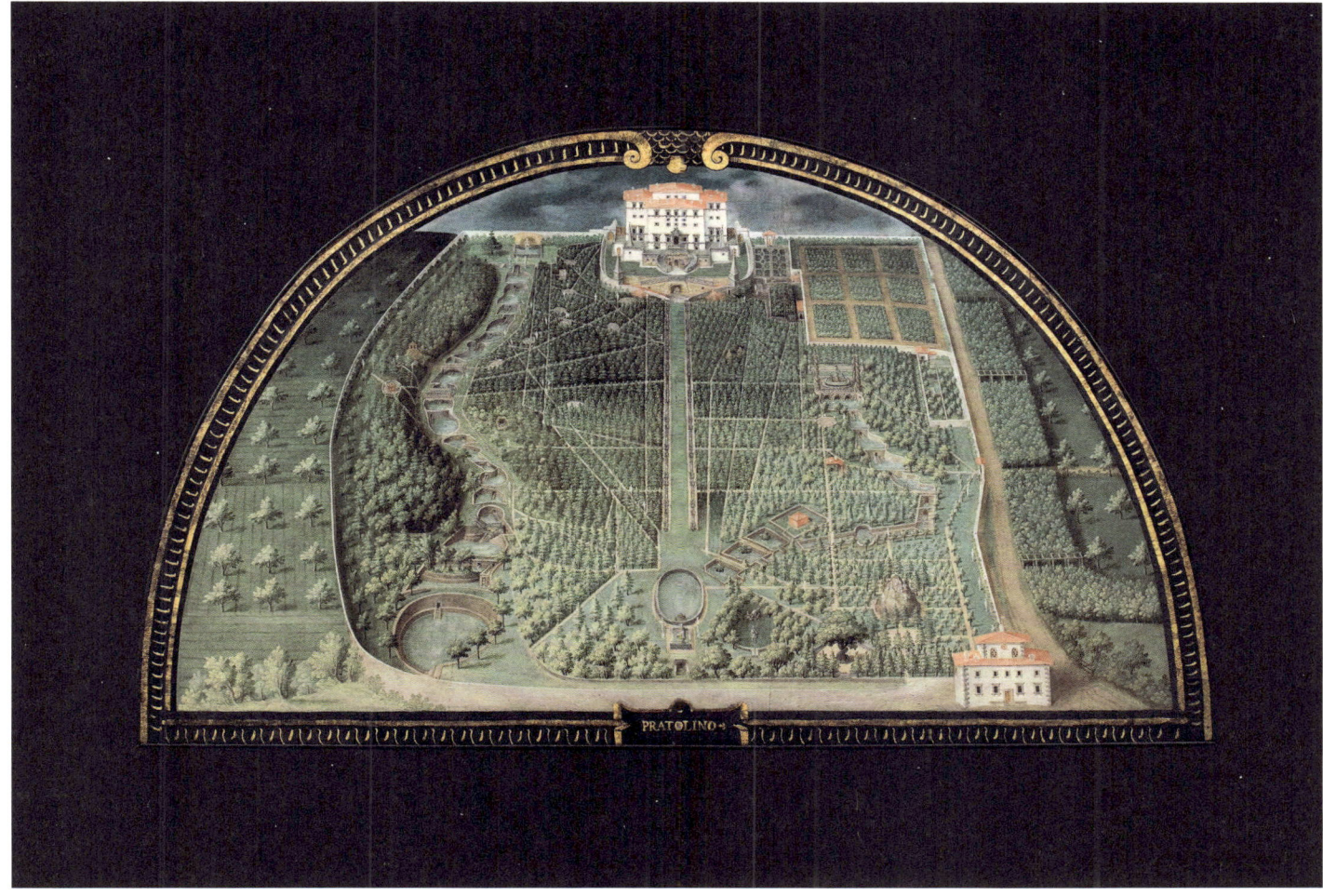

Fig 5 Giusto Utens, *Veduta della villa di Pratolino*, detail, 1599, painting

Fig 6 Stefano della Bella, *The Tree House at Pratolino*, sheet 1 of the series *Views of the Villa of Pratolino near Florence*, c. 1653, etching, Metropolitan Museum of Art, New York

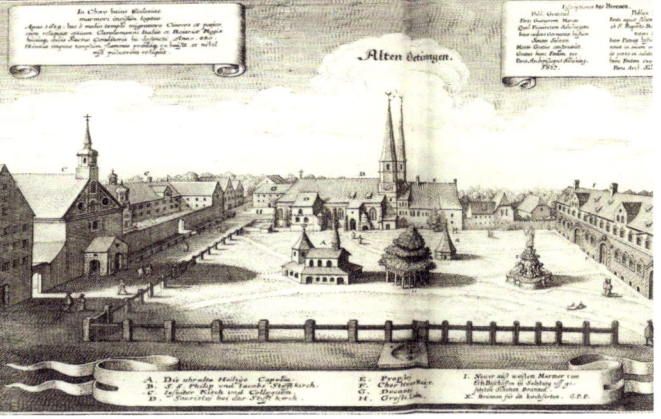

Fig 7 Matthäus Merian the Elder and Martin Zeiller, *View of Altötting*, from the *Topographia Bavariæ*, Vol. 4 of the *Topgraphia Germaniae*, 1664–1665, engraving

Fig 8 Hans Mielich for Orlando di Lasso, *4 Sacred songs*—1584, Staatsbibliothek München, Mus.ms. A II(1)

sixteenth century, particularly in the regions of Franconia, Thuringia, and Hesse, where people would meet under the *tanzlinden*, perpetuating a what was likely a Celtic tradition consolidated during the Holy Roman Empire (Fig 8). Girolamo Cardano (1501–1576) also gives an account of these structures in his *De Rerum Varietate*,[15] printed in Basel in 1557, in which he describes the great oak of Petersplatz in Basel, putting it in "competition" with the plane tree of Consul Gaius Licinius Mucianus described by Pliny; in 1473 the future Emperor Maximilian of Habsburg, at fourteen years old, stood under its branches.

Italy, with its *Signorie*, dictated the trend in garden design, and therefore in tree houses, throughout the sixteenth century and the early years of the seventeenth. The early-seventeenth-century mural attributed to Guercino's studio entitled *Casa di campagna con giardino e preparativi per colazione all'aperto* [Country house with garden and preparations for outdoor breakfast][16] (Fig 9), is a clear example. The mural shows the villa and a tree of equal standing, pruned like the architecture of the villa! In reality, the tree was not only pruned but was also scaffolded and transformed like the small pavilion in the villa of Castello.

With the extinction of the most important Italian Renaissance Courts, the cultural references for garden design changed, and especially in the French world, new models spread. Nonetheless, in the countries of northern Europe and in particular in England, the tradition remains linked to the Italian Renaissance garden for a longer period, continuing to build large plant structures throughout the sixteenth century. One example is the large "banqueting house," built by William Brook (1527–1597) on a lime tree at Cobham Hall; a complex structure, it is divided into three levels, each level eight feet higher than the one below. The tree's branches were pruned and scaffolded to seem "artfully made"; and were so tight and resistant that they supported boards on which fifty people could walk. The three "rooms" that occupied the different levels were connected by internal staircases.[17] John Evelyn (1620–1706), an English squire and one of the seventeenth century's more cultured authors, not only wrote a book about forestry, but also designed a structure in the park of his brother's house in Wotton, Surrey, which was accessed by a sinuous staircase, similar to that of Pratolino, connecting the ground to a platform partly covered by a small dome with a central pinnacle.[18] Another large house which was accessed by crossing a real entrance was that of Hampstead, reproduced in an engraving by Wenceslaus Hollar from 1653. It was a large elm, 28 feet in circumference at the ground level; at its highest point there was a 34-foot wide turret reached by climbing a 42-step spiral staircase dug into the trunk of the tree and illuminated by sixteen small windows. Six people could sit inside the 33-foot-high turret, while another fourteen could stand in a space next to it.[19] Aside from the tree structure's grandeur, the Hampstead house was of interest because it fused two types of houses: one on the tree and the other inside the tree. Another large house was Woburn in the Duke of Bedford's park, from which visitors could watch the deer hunt and admire the landscape.[20]

Clearly, for physiological reasons, these houses have all disappeared. However, in the village of Pitchford, in Shropshire, a Tudor-style house built on a lime tree that is considered the oldest tree house in the world, still stands. Its existence was documented in 1714 and it is included in the English Heritage list (Fig 10). The house has a square plan with the characteristic elements of the Tudor style: rendered in light plaster, visible load-bearing wooden elements, and Gothic-style elements adorning the windows' architraves and door.

The fashion for tree houses in England was eventually interrupted by the popularity of Capability Brown's English landscape garden. It is only later, with the concept of the "noble savage" developed in the philosophical theories of J. J. Rousseau, that tree houses had a revival, especially in France. In this same period, throughout Europe, garden design manuals became popular, dedicating many chapters to arboreal pergolas and "vegetable" pavilions. Of particular interest is the work of Louis-Eustache Audot (1783–1870),[21] who wrote a treatise to the *Arbre bélvèdere* and the *Arbre-maison* in which he presents four examples of tree houses (Fig 11). In literature, the family in *Der schweizerische Robinson*, or *The Swiss Family Robinson*, by Johann David Wyss,[22] lived in trees. The novel was a great success and helped renew interest in these structures. In 1848, Parc de l'île Robinson was built on the outskirts of Paris, where small houses were built on large chestnut trees to house restaurants which, at their peak, hosted up to 200 people (Fig 12).

Fig 9   Il Guercino and workshop, Casa di campagna con giardino e preparativi per colazione all'aperto, 1615–1617, mural, Civica Pinacoteca il Guercino di Cento

In France, and in particular in Normandy, we can still find centuries-old trees transformed into places of prayer. The Allouville Oak, known as Chêne Chapelle (Fig 13), is spectacular not only for its size and longevity, but also for the particular covering of the trunk with small oak slats, arranged in rows like roof tiles. The oak is 18 meters high with a circumference of 15 meters. Its inside is completely hollow and houses two small chapels, connected by a wooden staircase built on the outside of the trunk.

Approaching the end of our story, we cannot forget the 1914 manual by Phebe Westcott Humphreys, *Practical Book of Garden Architecture*, which dedicates an entire chapter on how to build tree houses. The text gives technical advice about how to choose the most suitable trees and how to make stair railings, etc.[23] Although this work, the first modern manual, was written by an American journalist, it is mainly in England that tree houses continued to be built. Architect Harold Peto, linked to the tradition of the Italian garden, designed in 1902 the tree house at Easton Lodge, Essex, for Daisy, Countess of Warwick. Named "Le Robinson" in homage to the Parisian tree restaurants, it was restored in 2009 and is open to visitors.

In the same period, Sir Thomas Lipton built a tearoom on his property in Osidge, Enfield,[24] on the outskirts of London, which brings to mind the tree house of Pratolino. The "room," built in a large oak tree, was reached by a spiral staircase that appears to be identical to the one reproduced in the sixteenth and seventeenth century works of Giusto Utens and Stefano della Bella. Despite the passing of centuries, the taste of "living" in trees had still not changed and we can only imagine the pleasure with which Sir Thomas Lipton sipped his tea in that natural room!

1- Italo Calvino, *Il Barone Rampante* (in English, *Baron in the Trees*) (Milan, 1957).

2- For further information see Roberta Martufi, *Abitare gli alberi fra terra e cielo. Dall'imperatore Caligola a Sir Thomas Lipton* (Naples, 2023).

3- Pliny the Elder, *Historia Naturalis*, Libro XII CAP. X.

4- Pliny the Elder, *Historia Naturalis*, Libro XII CAP. IX.

5- Jeroni Hieronymus Bosch, *Le tentazione di Sant' Antonio*, ca. 1500-1525, oil on canvas, 70" × 51", Madrid, Museo Nacional del Prado https://www.museodelprado.es/coleccion/obra-de-arte/las-tentaciones-de-san-antonio-abad/c1fb9065-66bd-4a6e-abd8-3b6a75431313

6- Pietro de Crescenzi, *De Ruralium Commodorum*, libri XII, B.N.C.F. ms. Pal. E.6.2.31, 1495.

7- Translated from the original by Sandra Persiani: "un palagio con caminate & camere di soli alberi nel quale possa dimorare il Re o la Reina co soi baroni o dône nel tempo asciuto & chiaro." De Crescenzi, *De Ruralium Commodorum*, Libro VIII, cap. III.

8- The incunabulum of the *Hyperotomachia Poliphili*, printed in Venice in 1469 by Aldo Manunzio and dedicated to Duke of Urbino Federico da Montefeltro, is kept in various Italian libraries. For a more convenient consultation, please refer to the anastatic print of the same. In particular: Francesco Colonna, *Hyperotomachia Poliphili*, edited by Marco Ariani and Mino Gabriele (Adelphi, 1998). The incunabulum has been defined as the most beautiful book of the Italian Renaissance, perhaps still not completely "deciphered" in its deepest meaning.

9- Giorgio Vasari, *Le vite de' più eccellenti pittori, scultori e architettori* (Florence, 1878-1885).

10- Michel de Montaigne, *Viaggio in Italia* (Bari, 1991), 139.

11- Translated from the original by Sandra Persiani. "… vi era un bosco con tutte le apparenze di una casa fatta con artificiosa mano di maestro. La onde vi era sala, camera, cucina, dispensa, et camere tutte queste stanze erano ricoperte di verzure e di varie fronde di diverse piante di più vi vedrai un tavolino in sala nel cui mezzo vi viene acqua cristallina si per bere altresì per bagnare i convitati dopo il banchetto per spasso e scherzo."

Agostino del Riccio, *Agricoltura Teorica*, vol. I c 27r, BNC di Florence, MS Targioni Tozzetti.

12- de Montaigne, *Viaggio in Italia*, 43.

13- Fynes Moryson, *The Itinerary*, volume I (Glasgow: James MacLehose and Sons Publishers to the University, 1907), 50-51.

14- de Montaigne, *Viaggio in Italia*, 43.

15- Girolamo Cardano, *De Rerum Varietate*, Liber VI, cap. XXII (Avignon, 1588), 166.

16- https://bbcc.ibc.regione.emilia-romagna.it/pater/loadcard.do?id_card=158297&force=1

17- John Parckinson, *Paradisi in Sole, Paradisus Terrestre* (London: Methuen & Co., 1904).

18- British Library, H. [John Evelyn?]: *View of Wotton with the garden, grotto and environs from the western corner*; [1650s?], Add MS 78610 H.

19- *The Gentleman's Magazine, and Historical Chronicle*, Vol LXXXV, 436. John Claudius Loudon, *Arboretum et fruticetum britannicum* (London, 1838), 1391.

20- Celia Fiennes, *The Journeys of Celia Fiennes, (1685-1703)* (1983), 140.

21- L. E. Audot, *Traité de la composition et de l'ornement des jardins : avec cent soixante et une planches représentant, en plus de six cent figures, des plans de jardins, des fabriques propres à leur décoration, et des machines pour élever les eaux ; ouvrage faisant suite à l'Almanach du bon jardinier*, (Paris, 1859), vol. I, 99-100; Vol. II, plate 26, fig. 3.

22- Johann David Wyss, *Der schweizerische Robinson* (Zurich, 1812).

23- For further information on Phebe Westcott Humphreys, see Paula Henderson and Adam Mornement, *Treehouses* (Frances Lincoln Ltd, 2005), 36-38; and Courtney McKinney, *Treehouses: Civilizing the Wildness of Men and Nature*, English Undergraduate Distinction Projects. https://scholar.smu.edu/hum_sci_english_distinction/1, 2018, 59.

24- For further information, see Henderson and Mornement, *Treehouses*, 36-41.

Fig 10 Pitchford Hall, Shropshire, a Tudor-style house built into a great seventeenth-century lime tree

Fig 11 Audot, L.-E., *Traité de la composition et de l'ornement des jardins: avec cent soixante et une planches représentant, en plus de six cent figures, des plans de jardins, des fabriques propres à leur décoration, et des machines pour élever les eaux; ouvrage faisant suite à l'Almanach du bon jardinier*, L'arbre Maison de Matibò, Vol. II, plate 26, fig. 3

Fig 12 The restaurant Le Vraie Arbre de Robinson in Le Plessis-Robinson, France

Fig 13 The oak of the chapel of Notre-Dame-de-la-Ronce in Allouville-Bellefosse, France

Taming the Garden, a documentary film by Salomé Jashi, 2021

Salomé Jashi

A TREE IS NOT JUST A TREE
Making the Film *Taming the Garden*

In this review Georgian filmmaker Salomé Jashi tells a powerful story about what trees can mean to a society and how they are depicted while working on the documentary *Taming the Garden*. It also recounts the political effect the film had in Georgia.

In *Taming the Garden*, the documentary released in 2021, I tried to embody the concept of uprooting and to translate a tangible reality into a universal metaphor.

In 2016, a wealthy and powerful man, who is also the former prime minister of Georgia, developed an exquisite hobby. He decided to collect century-old, large trees along Georgia's coastline. He commissioned his men to uproot these trees and to bring them to his garden, his park. Some of these trees were as tall as fifteen-floor-buildings. In order to transplant trees of such dimensions, other trees were chopped down, electric cables were shifted, the railway was stopped, and new roads were paved. The trees were taken from forests, villages, and family yards.

The road to the park lay through the Black Sea.

When I first saw this image—of a large tree floating in the sea—it seemed like a glitch. It was an image that wasn't supposed to be there; a sudden, unexpected glimpse into a different world. The sea is serene. Waves gently stroke the shore. It's a cloudy midday. And there on the horizon, somewhere in the distance a tall, erect tree swims. It was a mesmerizing, beautiful image. I watched it live thinking of how Bidzina Ivanishvili, that wealthy and politically powerful man, had made this perfect piece of art, proving that even the impossible is possible.

But this image was also a manifestation of power and a desire to be satisfied at any cost. It spoke of uprooting, not of just trees, but of beliefs, values, cultures, and people. It spoke of migration, the human migration forced by wars, repressions, economic hardships. It also made me think of loneliness, abandonment, longing, greed, and masculinity.

In short, this single image was charged with so many connotations and metaphors, it symbolized so much. At that time the tree floating in the sea was a liriodendron. It stirred my heart, messed up my mind, and I thought I must explore what is behind this singular picture, what's inside this glitch. I must document it, and see if I can convey these initial sensations through a film.

Taming the Garden is a documentary film, but it definitely is not a documentation. The making of it took four years. During this period a total of 200 trees were removed from private and public estates and took the journey to the garden. As if people had suddenly discovered treasure in their yards. Trees had become a convertible currency, and their owners were trying to trade it for much desired cash. Considering that over 20 percent of Georgia's population lived in absolute poverty in those years (2016–2020), you can only imagine how many were searching and measuring the trees in their yards.

Trees have always been a central element of a rural Georgian household. A traditional Georgian family, usually consisting of three generations, lives in their ancestral home, which includes a fenced yard with a house in the center. A vegetable garden lies behind the house and a central tree stands in front of it, in bright sight from the front gate. These central trees are usually said to be planted by great-grandparents or someone in the family, who first built the house. In Georgian we call this concept "Pudze," which is similar to the word "roots," "foundation," or "base," something stable you stand on or build on; but it mostly has an abstract meaning, it's not necessarily physical.

I took my camera and made several research trips to Georgia's coastline to find connections and do some test filming. We explored the locations from where trees were supposed to be taken. Those were eucalyptuses, magnolias, oaks, limes, chestnuts, and other large trees. We learned that Bidzina Ivanishvili would personally visit them to give approval and that he was particularly keen on the large root systems extending in the ground.

Bidzina Ivanishvili, a multibillionaire, kept a radically low profile for most of his life. Even his photograph could not be found anywhere. He would finance some parts of culture, he paid wages of Georgia's parliament members, he sponsored the construction of the country's largest church. He was an anonymous, mysterious figure, a collector of expensive pieces of art and exotic animals. In 2012 he showed his face and decided to come to power. He established a political party called Georgian Dream, won majority seats in the parliament, became the prime minister only to resign in a year. Since then, Bidzina Ivanishvili has been the shadow ruler of the country. With no tangible responsible position, he is behind all political and economic decisions.

However, the film does not tell just Ivanishvili's story as such. In fact, his name is hardly mentioned. We tried to put the film together as a universal story where money can buy anything and trees are just an example, an embodiment of this "anything," which includes both the material and the immaterial. I remember how I felt when I first saw a tree move. It was night. We were standing with a rolling camera in anticipation of the main action.

And there, as the tree slid and shook in the manner I had never seen before, I suddenly felt dizzy and nauseous, as if my axis had shifted. My reaction was not an intellectual judgment or a feeling from the heart, it was purely physical. This sensation and others like it very much shaped the film, as for me film as a language is not just a collection of images, but it is the connotations those images and sounds carry and create together or individually.

There is no straightforward development line in *Taming the Garden*. As we were putting the film together with editor Chris Wright, we agreed on the starting point—the trees are already moving, the reality has already flipped, there is nothing to lean on, this is not an ordinary world as we know it anymore. And then it was about finding the right pieces of the puzzle, not to necessarily give a full picture, which was quite impossible, but to give hints, indications, details. So the audience could build or imagine the totality in their heads and hearts.

We constructed the film with two elements—dialogues and so-called pillar shots. Chris was great at putting together bits of spoken words that we then scattered in the film to have a gradual, unimpeded introduction of some context and reactions. I am tempted to say facts, but in this film, there are no facts. In this story, there are no facts. In the use of spoken words and the visual elements, we embraced mythical storytelling, where nothing is certain, nothing can be proven and pinned down. It's a world out of balance.

The pillar shots are standalone shots that speak hardly of what you directly see in them. Composed with attention to detail, these shots are charged with meanings and evocations, sometimes explicit, sometimes less tangible. As we were editing, and filming, we would try to exclude purely descriptive images. However, nice and beautiful they looked, an image, an action was worthless if it didn't mean anything, if it didn't carry a wider connotation, if it didn't work as a metaphor beyond.

Putting the film together was like balancing on a thin rope. We did not want to explain too much, and we did not want to give too little either. It should be a door open just wide enough to give a glimpse of just exactly enough to imagine, to trigger curiosity and a thought process. Making *Taming the Garden* was like constructing a game, an alternative world with some rules. Rules imply exclusion. Excluding anything that diverts attention is part of the creation. However, I am sad that some stories remained "behind the fences," as people restrained themselves from sharing. They were afraid of the billionaire's power exercised through local governments, influential in Georgia's provinces. For them speaking of trees meant speaking of politics and of the influence of Bidzina Ivanishvili. To me, too, trees were a medium, a variable.

Exclusion also meant leaving out much of the side process behind the frame—the engineering, environmental aspects, politics, violation of laws, and the fact that finally the park is open to the public, but remains privately owned by the Ivanishvili family.

One of the rules we set ourselves was that the camera must always be static—it's not our camera, our point of view that moves, but that of the trees. Thus, the center of movement is accentuated, and the subject of movement is reversed.

Soon we discovered that it was difficult to predict the dimensions of trees as they were driven. Sure, we could predict the dimensions of a human and consider this prediction in our placement of the camera. But curiously, with trees, we could never tell how they would fill the space in a shot when they traversed the composition. This could have been one of the triggers that made me acknowledge relativity of scale as one of the central elements, or tendencies, in the film. Here a human is the smallest in scale. In the film they are often small and far, especially when seen with the larger machines, excavators, which, on their part, are smaller than the trees. And the trees themselves are minor, tiny in comparison to the sea where they journey. And what is the sea in comparison to the desire of the rich and mighty man?

"This magnificent tree, so fertile, with its moss . . . It's shrunk so much," says an elderly woman as she watches a chestnut being driven away at night. Someone replies that it feels shrunken because the workers have trimmed the branches, but she insists— it's the actual trunk that seems smaller to her. This was such a special example of a visual and mental illusion. While the physical parameters of the trunk surely remained the same, the tree was grandiose only in its natural habitat and it lost its scape, its value, after uprooting.

Building relativities was also very much part of the sound design. Working with Philip Ciompi, we embraced the dichotomy of silence and loudness. The noise made by the machines was like a violent invasion into the silence of nature, or natural, life. We tried to animate trees and their movements. I am particularly thinking of an oak being driven in an alley at night, where it "plays piano" with the standing trees, pushing them like keys, in both the audio and visual sense. The rhythm that the machines offered was also an inspiration for music carefully selected and put together or readjusted by Celia Stroom.

Making *Taming the Garden* and releasing it was a unique and adventurous journey. Without the collaboration of each one of the team members, this film would have been different. I need to acknowledge the researcher Tamara Mshvenieradze, with whom we covered a multitude of locations across Georgia's coastline and multiple people involved in the process. I should also mention co-cinematographer Goga Devdariani, with whom we shaped the visual approach; we "saw" the film together.

Taming the Garden could never really be released on a big screen in Georgia. A leading politician called it a shameful film and the Minister of Culture called it a lie, both of them defending or rather whitewashing Bidzina Ivanishvili, their political leader. They were upset the film did not show how the park was now open to the public, arguing that this endeavor was made only for the public benefit. This accusation makes me wonder about what is private and what is public in a country where a multibillionaire owns the politics, the economy, and the public sphere. It also makes me wonder about filmmaking in general: what is a truth and what is a lie. Is there truth as such and is there a lie as such in the process of constructing, imagining a film, which is some individual's artistic vision?

The attack on *Taming the Garden* was not singular. By the time the film came out, the government was already exercising pressure on independent cultural actors and institutions. It attacked freedom of expression and civil society. As a case of actual censorship and criticism by the government and those affiliated, *Taming the Garden* became famous in Georgia and was brought to the frontline of the fight for independent creativity and culture. Variations of the film title—"Taming the culture," "We won't be tamed," "Untamed"—emerged in the media, becoming a shorthand reference to the moment. The slogans also reference and bring alive the 1983 Soviet-era book by Georgian writer Akaki Bakradze *Taming Literature*, one of the inspirations for the film title.

Fig 1 An oak, sitting on a flatbed, is transported across the sea. It comes from a household yard in the village Didi Nedzi-Kakhati in Samegrelo and is heading towards the park in Shekvetili. By the coast of Anaklia, 2019.

Fig 2 Workers rake fallen leaves in the garden. Trees are held with wires to the earth to sustain stability in their new home. Bidzina Ivanishvili family estate, Shekvetili Dendrological Park, 2019.

Fig 3 A linden tree in front of a family house in the village Darcheli, Mingrelia. The family refused to sell the tree. The shot was not included in the final cut of the film, 2019.

Fig 4 The village inhabitants reluctantly start following a tree as it is taken away, 2019.

Fig 5 A family in the village Didi Nedzi-Kakhati discusses the possibility of cutting down their tree, which stands in the way of the transport of the large tree to the Shekvetili park, 2019.

Fig 6 Pipes are inserted deep in the soil one after another under a tree, disjoining soil with the roots from the rest of the earth. Large iron bars are then put under the pipes, the tree is lifted, and the soil is cleared underneath the pipes and the tree to make way for a flatbed to drive under it. In the village Laituri, 2018.

Fig 7   Water runs across the barge floor after a tree is loaded on it, 2019.

Fig 8   The top of a eucalyptus is cut down. The tree stands in the way of another eucalyptus to be transported, 2019.

Fig 9   The barge hits the beach. An oak will be loaded on it, 2019.

Fig 10   The film starts with smoke entering a village from which a tree will soon be removed. The smoke forms a whirlpool, 2019.

Fig 11   Towards the end of the film a whirlpool appears again, this time in the water, where the tree is about to swim, 2019.

Fig 12 Workers cut down trees to clear way for machines to enter into the forest to start removing a tree, 2017.

Fig 13 A tree approaching the pier close to Shekvetili park in early morning, 2019.

Fig 14 An oak is driven through an alley of trees outside the village Laituri, Guria, Georgia, 2018.

One Hundred and Fifty Thousand Trees by White Arkitekter, 2023

Hannes Harter and Michael Vollmer in Conversation with Ferdinand Ludwig and Kristina Pujkilović

TREES AND TIMBER:
A Life Cycle Perspective

As the founders of vesta sustainability consulting, Michael Vollmer and Hannes Harter are dedicated to promoting sustainable building practices. They do this by applying a holistic method that takes the entire life cycle of buildings into account and promises to have environmentally, economically, and socially positive impacts. Their role in *Trees, Time, Architecture!* was to calculate the exhibition's total carbon emissions. In this conversation with Kristina Pujkilović and Ferdinand Ludwig, Michael and Hannes discuss the lifespan of buildings in relation to the growth rate of trees and explore the question of whether slow-growing trees can really meet the rising demand for timber as an ecologically sound material in the long term. This conversation is complemented by a sequence of stills from the film *One Hundred and Fifty Thousand Trees* by White Arkitekter.

Ferdinand: When speaking about the life cycle of buildings, the first question that arises is what the life expectancy of a building *should* be.

Michael: The longer, the better in principle, as quickly becomes clear when you start drafting life cycle analyses. Historically, buildings often had a long lifespan for the simple reason that resources were precious. Yet many of the buildings that went up in West Germany during its postwar "economic miracle" were built on the assumption that we had virtually limitless resources at our disposal. Not surprisingly, many of those structures turned out to be short-lived. Shoddy materials meant that many of them had to be renovated or demolished long before their time.

Ferdinand: So, what *is* the lifespan of a building on which your ideas are premised? Can you give me a number?

Hannes: Fifty years.

Kristina: That doesn't sound like much.

Hannes: No, indeed! There are many examples of buildings that remain perfectly usable for far longer than that. Of course, buildings have to be looked after and properly maintained; that is essential to any extension of their lifespan. And ecologically speaking, it makes sense to maintain existing structures, given the amount of energy and materials that went into their construction. The substance of a building should be preserved for as long as possible, though its function can of course change.

Ferdinand: Half a century may sound short, but when we think of the world fifty years from now, we realize that it is beyond the scope of what we can realistically imagine. So, a building's end-of-life has to be one of the many scenarios you work with—and what then? What interested us in connection with *Trees, Time, Architecture!* is the question of wood, that is timber, as a building material: Should it be incinerated or recycled elsewhere? To me, it is a purely speculative question, given how uncertain the future is. How do you cope with this uncertainty when imagining a building's end?

> Michael: True, it is purely speculative, but when calculating the life cycle assessments required for certification systems, we are bound by certain specifications from regulations, norms or certification systems, including end-of-life scenarios for the materials being used. The database we use for this in Germany is the ÖKOBAUDAT database, according to which timber is disposed of "thermally;" in other words, it is incinerated. This, then, has to be the premise for our building certifications. Outside such systems, however, there are alternative scenarios that can be considered. If a building is torn down fifty years hence, there is no reason why materials like wooden beams cannot be reused.

> Hannes: What matters is to allow for a range of possible future scenarios. Those who may decide to dismantle a building in the future should at least be given the chance to cleanly separate its constituent materials. We should not be taking the attitude that "fifty years is too far in the future for us to predict, so why should we care what happens then?"

Ferdinand: This is turning into an extremely interesting discussion, especially as the issue is basically a building's ecological footprint. This is a subject that you addressed in your dissertation, Michael, where you described buildings as "laying claim to ecosystems." What did you mean by that?

> Michael: I took a building as a case study and calculated its total emissions over a period of fifty years from the production of the building materials along its operation to its end of life. My focus was not just on carbon dioxide but also on eutrophication and acidification. I then analyzed these data in relation to Germany's ecosystems, meaning its forests, grassland, heath, moor, swamp, and bodies of water, in order to calculate the level of emissions that those ecosystems would be able to absorb without incurring long-term damage. Last, but not least, I calculated the emissions of a building and broke them down to a single year in order to ascertain the total land area of such ecosystems that would be needed to absorb the said annual emissions.

Ferdinand: But when your findings are extrapolated to construction in Germany as a whole, it soon becomes clear that its ecological footprint is far greater than the land area needed to absorb it. This, of course, gives pause for thought, as well as making offsets in the form of foreign reforestation projects look all the more attractive.

> Michael: In theory, yes. But first we have to look into which emissions are avoidable, since emissions that do not occur in the first place do not have to be reduced or offset at all. The second step should be to look into efficiency measures. Offsets, in other words, should always be the last resort. My study also showed that if we continue to build in the conventional way, Germany will simply not have sufficiently large ecosystems to offset the resulting emissions.

Ferdinand: Your best case is a solid timber structure that counts as sustainable by today's standards. The data obtained from this are a lot better, so it could be argued that we are moving in the right direction. Except that the timber has to come from somewhere, which brings us back to the topic of the forest. So, we put our heads together to calculate how big a forest would be needed over the lifespan of a building and arrived at a very large forest indeed. This, in its turn, raised a controversial question: If building with timber, which now counts as best practice, were adopted globally, would we even have the resources—the forests—needed for that?

> Hannes: The reason I'm no fan of absolutist approaches such as a switch to one-hundred-percent timber is that they disregard other important aspects, such as biodiversity and the preservation of natural habitats. When it comes to life cycle assessments, however, the fact is that building with timber is currently the best choice with respect to both its life cycle as a material and its carbon dioxide emissions. At the same time, we should not waver in our decarbonization of the energy supply, as the carbon emissions from the production of materials such as steel and concrete are going to have to be a lot lower in the future.

Ferdinand: The forest converts solar energy into wood at an efficiency rate of less than 3 percent. The latest solar cells, by contrast, reach efficiency rates of more than 30 percent. Using this energy source for steel production would result in a much higher building output per square meter than would building with timber alone. This begs the question: Could materials made with solar energy be ecologically better than one-hundred-percent natural timber? Timber is currently regarded as the only readily available resource that might adequately substitute for harmful materials like reinforced concrete. But we have to watch the situation closely as this could well change in future years.

Kristina: I would like to move away from this general discussion of building with timber to the very specific question raised by our exhibition. As you know, we are planning to calculate its carbon footprint. One key issue for us is what to include in our calculation.

Michael: Defining the boundaries of the system to determine what should and should not be included is crucial to any life cycle assessment. If the system is an exhibition, we have to assume that the rooms will have to be heated, dehumidified, and ventilated. The exhibits themselves are also relevant, meaning that the emissions from the production and disposal of a canvas, say, will also have to be part of the equation. Another factor is transport. How and from where are the exhibits being shipped? And what about the means of transport used by people visiting the exhibition? There are inevitably many such debatable points, given that the goal is to produce an honest and plausible life cycle assessment.

Ferdinand: My hypothesis is that the materials used for the exhibition architecture, which incidentally we chose with care to ensure that they can be recycled and reused, will account for a much smaller share of the total than the emissions from transport, travel, and the use of the building. If we ran the exhibition for only half the time planned so that the building were used less, we could probably save more resources than if we concentrated exclusively on using sustainable materials for the exhibition architecture. I'm eager to see what the data actually say on this and whether we will be able to test this hypothesis.

Kristina: Irrespective of where the system boundaries are drawn, we nevertheless intend to offset all the unavoidable emissions. You described that as a last resort, Michael, which is why instead of relying on dubious certificates from abroad, we intend to use Munich's tree clippings to make coal. The idea is to find out how much carbon is already locked inside the trees. While some of this carbon will be released when the tree clippings are carbonized, some of it will remain permanently bonded. If this material

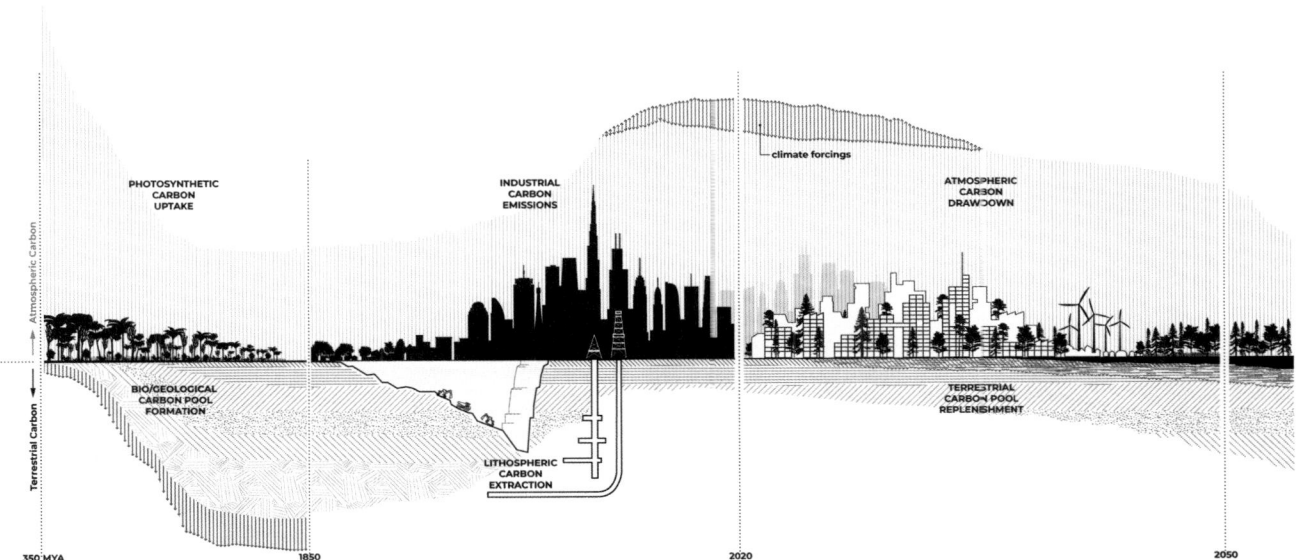

Global CO$_2$ concentration, formation, and use of coal in relation to forest development and architecture over different time periods.
© GOA Architecture

is then worked into the soil, the carbon will remain stored there for centuries. Obviously, we will have to produce an enormous quantity of coal for this. In fact, if everyone were to do the same, we would simply not have enough land available to grow the biomass needed for such carbon offsets.

Ferdinand: Which goes to show how important it is, and how challenging, to weigh up the options available to us, as you did in your doctoral dissertation, Michael. Many are now claiming that trees and carbon offsets from urban green spaces will save us. This is where *Baubotanik* comes in, which is why it was allotted a whole room to itself in the exhibition. It is often argued that living trees in buildings continue bonding carbon dioxide throughout their entire lifespan. While that is certainly not wrong, the carbon-offsetting capacity of green building materials and even green spaces is trivial in relation to global carbon dioxide levels. We must differentiate between the global and the local. Trees are important at the local level, as a way of both adapting to climate change and improving air quality; but cultivating trees just to make a carbon footprint look better is really just greenwashing. That is why the exhibition treats these as two separate issues. We start with carbon dioxide and then deliberately touch on the subject of building with wood—though as we said at the outset, there are conflicts here that have to do with the lifespan of trees and the question of whether they grow fast enough. We then show how the forest is becoming an industrial-scale producer before switching to the theme of the local climate.

Hannes: Most important of all is to bear in mind the following: The emissions we are causing today will endure for decades. Even if we stopped emitting anything at all right now, the climate would still continue changing, unperturbed. It seems to me that although the time factor is being discussed, it is not being tackled pragmatically. We have the methods, but all too often end up repeating the same processes and so missing the potential for change.

Michael: Time is indeed an interesting subject in this context. The impact of emissions on climate is generally felt only ten years down the line. The positive effects of any measures adopted today, in other words, will be felt only in the future. Even if we were to generate "negative emissions" today, we would still have to wait ten years to notice any effect. What matters is that we work on positive solutions instead of worrying about trivial things such as the size of the latest smart phone. We must become more acutely aware of the fact that we are wholly dependent on nature.

Kristina: Which brings us in closing to the subtitle of the exhibition, which is *Design in Constant Transformation*. The ambiguity of the concept of "transformation" is what matters most here. Not only do we have to radically rethink and constantly review our style of designing, planning, and building, but we must also be willing to develop and transform what we already have, whether in the way we use it or the usability of the materials.

Vesta sustainability consulting has determined the CO_2 emissions of the exhibition *Trees, Time, Architecture!*. The report is available via this QR code or here: www.arc.ed.tum.de/en/gtla/trees-time-architecture/

Right page:
One Hundred and Fifty Thousand Trees by White Arkitekter

Architecture plays a complicit role in environmental degradation, social inequality, and energy imbalance. *One Hundred and Fifty Thousand Trees*, produced for the 2023 Venice Architecture Biennale, hints at the risks involved in our misinterpretation of complex entanglements, the reductive view of nature, and numerical approaches to landscape management. Can a balance be found between the forest as a resource and the urgent need for fragile ecologies to be preserved and rebuilt?

Our installation unpacks a recent timber project from Skellefteå, Sweden, exploring building technology, material supply chains, and their impact on the forests from which it was built. Sara Cultural Centre (Sara Kulturhus), completed in 2021, is a symbol for sustainable timber architecture and is a perfect case study for dissection. Using carbon as an agreed measure and currency, the workshop allows us to unpick the politics of "zero" and point towards positive new forms of practice.

Team:
Jake Ford, Elena Kanevsky, David Clark

Technical collaborators:
Clara Terne (digital artist), Martin Lang (Lang Film, cinematographer and editor), Pär Olofsson (cinematographer), Oliver Börnfelt (sound engineer), Magnus Lewrén (Lewrén Produktion, video technician)

Inclusion point on the Plane Tree Cube. Note how the ever-larger shoots have slowly but surely overwhelmed the steel tubes and cross bolts.

Ferdinand Ludwig, Daniel Schönle, and Jakob Rauscher

THE MAKING OF LIVING ARCHITECTURE
How to Design with Trees and Time

How can trees become buildings? How can the crown of a tree become a habitat for humans? And how can urban transformation processes be tied to the growth of trees? These are the questions that the Office for Living Architecture (OLA) asks itself in pursuit of its mission to find new ways of putting the spatial, aesthetic, environmental, structural, and processual potential of trees to fruitful use in architecture, urban development, and landscaping. Here, the founders of OLA, Ferdinand Ludwig, Daniel Schönle, and Jakob Rauscher, explain where the opportunities and challenges of arboreal architecture lie, citing selected *Baubotanik* projects as examples.

BAUBOTANIK—DESIGNING AND BUILDING WITH TREES

As adherents of Baubotanik, we endeavor to create architecture made with and of trees. We use trees as load-bearing and stiffening elements, to create spaces, to influence the microclimate, and to improve the ecological equilibrium. The term *Baubotanik* was first coined at the University of Stuttgart's Institute for Principles of Modern Architecture (IGMA) in 2007. After ten years of research at the IGMA, the subject was established at the Technical University of Munich (TUM) with the creation of the Professorship for Green Technologies in Landscape Architecture. The integration of Baubotanik into landscape architecture comes as no surprise, given the field's long tradition of designing with living systems. Baubotanik builds on that tradition as well as on a long history of its own, given that humanity has been shaping and grafting trees, branches, and roots since time immemorial.

The tree has two roles to play here, being at once an object of planning that has to obey the same structural logic as non-organic building materials, and an active, to a certain extent autonomous, subject. This means that its future form and structure cannot be prescribed since they arise out of the tree's own interactions with both its surroundings and human interventions (care and maintenance work) over time.

Our design practice at the Office for Living Architecture (OLA) is informed by three different approaches to designing with time. The first of these is the purely horticultural approach in which a small tree is planted and over the decades trained and manipulated to form a particular structure. The second is the constructive approach, in which a tree of certain dimensions is purchased—the price tag depending on the years it spent in the nursery—as a living building material. The third approach, which we call "plant addition," involves using young trees to create structures that slowly grow together and eventually form a single, collective organism. Right from the outset, the entire structure has the green volume of a fully grown tree.[1]

The Plane-Tree Cube in Nagold was the first public, and to date the largest, built project to which the latter approach of plant addition was brought to bear. The 10 × 10-meter cube, which was erected in the town of Nagold in the Black Forest as part of a garden show in 2012, was conceived as a long-term experiment in Baubotanik and urban development. It began with the creation of the "green walls": some 1,200 young plane trees in pots arranged on six levels to create a space open to the sky. Platforms for visitors are set up on three different levels inside this space and are accessed via single-flight steel staircases. The whole structure is supported by vertical steel supports that will be removed as soon as the plant structure has become sturdy enough to become a load-bearing structure. The platforms are attached to the steel frame, which in turn is designed so that loads can be transmitted to the plant structure at several different points. As the building matures and the trees develop crowns, the space will gradually close to the sky, while in the lower parts, the tree trunks become larger, gnarly and more prominent. During the garden show, the cube served as both a viewing platform and as a shady retreat. Once the show was over, it was integrated into the grounds of a newly built childcare center as part of Nagold's urban growth. In the first few years, the progress of the project was determined by the adaptation and further development of the vegetation technology systems, which had to withstand extreme demands due to public use and the harsh weather conditions at the edge of the Black Forest. Subsequently, the plants developed vigorously with strong thickness growth and good development of the baubotanical nodes.

BRAIDING TIMELINES

The example of the Plane-Tree Cube shows that in Baubotanik, the parameter of time has to be factored in not just at the design level but earlier, at the conceptual level. Because it is there that the standard question that all architecture has to answer—which goals are to be achieved with which methods and materials—is joined by the *when*: When will the desired objectives be achieved and how will the period in-between be handled? Does a project start with the act of planting or the act of building? Will the important objectives be met right away or only years or even decades hence? Should the functions that the plants are one day to fulfill be anticipated by temporary, technical support structures or architectural means until that day is reached? Are the objectives likely to develop and change over time? It follows that Baubotanik projects should always be developed with a view to the adaptation and transformation of those ecosystems and urban structures of which they are to form an integral part. After all, how they inscribe themselves into the urban fabric or landscape setting will differ, depending on which approach to time is taken. It is therefore vital to enable a fruitful relationship between tree growth and urban growth and between slowness and speed, even if urban development is often very fast when viewed in relation to the growth of trees.

The Prato in Caelo project design developed by OLA,[2] which won second prize in the 2016 competition for a new city park in Prato, Italy, demonstrated how Baubotanik can accompany, influence, and upgrade an urban transformation process. The brief was to remodel the site of a former hospital as a public green space, and the development process that OLA proposed for this was akin to a dramatization of the step-by-step demolition of the hospital and the opening of the site to the public. The underlying assumption was that the constantly changing relationship between the emergent park and the growth of its green structures would be exciting to watch. The focus, therefore, was not on any predefined park design but on the experience of following a never-ending process of transformation.

Topographical and architectural elements from various previous phases of use were to be retained, transformed, and rendered legible. The design proposal is characterized by several iconic baubotanical towers that complement the skyline of Prato, which is dominated by numerous buildings of very different heights, in a unique way. These "tree towers," consisting of both baubotanical structures and the former hospital's access shafts, were to forge a symbolic link between the site's past and future. The trees needed for this were to be cultivated in a nursery in a publicly accessible part of the park. After about three years, applying the plant addition method, these would have been mounted at various heights on the towers and connected with each other. After ten to twenty years, they would have fused together to form a single organism capable of drawing its own nutrients from the soil. In future years, the mature structures with their concrete cores—from the remains of the hospital—would have continued to bear witness to Prato's deep-rooted social, cultural, ecological, and economic transformation.

OUTLOOK

More than twenty years have passed since the landscape architect Gilles Clément published his groundbreaking ecological manifesto *The Planetary Garden*.[3] Calling on humanity to tend and cultivate the planet entrusted to its care just as lovingly as a gardener tends and cultivates a garden, Clément argued that it was vital that we work with, and not against, the principles underpinning nature's own ecosystems, as only then would we be able to preserve the complexity and diversity of life.[4] Looking at today's cities, however, we generally see the exact opposite. Dominating the picture are buildings and infrastructure built to global standards without heed for either local ecosystems or the surrounding countryside. Some cities are planned well and are interlaced with a system of parks and tree-lined avenues,[5] however, green spaces are often merely residual areas that offer little space for

Pre-cultivated baubotanical elements being mounted on the Plane-Tree Cube.

Projected development shows the plants growing together to form a single organism and, with it, a self-supporting structure.

The Plane-Tree Cube in Nagold several years after completion

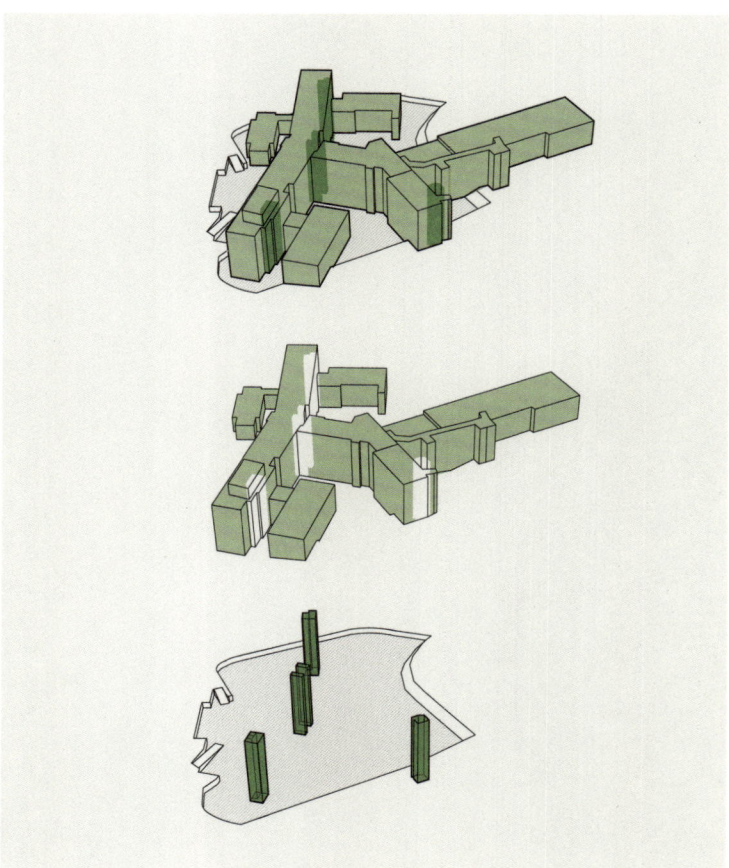

Baubotanik concept for the transformation of the Prato in Caelo park, premised on the hospital access shafts being retained when the rest of the complex is demolished.

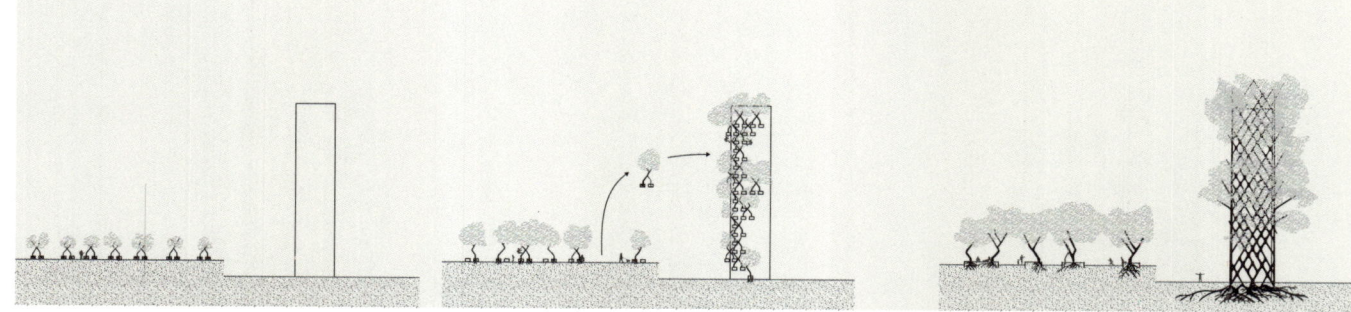

Pre-cultivation, selection, assembly, and development of baubotanical building elements for the Prato in Caelo towers

Visualization of the botanically built towers with the remaining access shafts in the foreground and the former nursery in the background

planting trees or designing high-quality gardens. If we are to take Clément's message to heart, we must start regarding buildings, too, not as foreign bodies but as integral parts of our planetary garden. They should therefore be developed to engender a symbiotic relationship between the technical and the biological. Baubotanik is merging buildings and trees to create a new whole, allowing us to hope that this can indeed be accomplished.

It should nevertheless be remembered that the constant attentiveness and care that Clément demands of the "planetary gardener" are just as essential to Baubotanik projects, which also have to be actively looked after throughout their entire life cycle. Whatever care concepts are applied, moreover, they have to be continuously reviewed and adapted to the prevailing circumstances. While this is nothing new in landscape architecture and horticulture, to architects it might seem like an unwarranted imposition. Yet it is an imposition that we must have the courage to face if we are to develop a processual approach to tackling the environmental and social challenges posed by accelerating climate change. Armed with such courage, what might at first have felt like an imposition could become an opportunity for tapping the environmental and aesthetic potential of trees to create life-friendly and forward-looking buildings and cities.

1- Ferdinand Ludwig and Daniel Schönle, *Growing Architecture: How to Design and Build with Trees* (Basel: Birkhäuser, 2023).

2- In collaboration with: umschichten, allmannsattlerwappner, Sergio Sanna, Carlo Scoccianti, green4cities.

3- Gilles Clément, *"The Planetary Garden" and Other Writings* (Philadelphia: University of Pennsylvania Press, 2015).

4- Clément, *"The Planetary Garden."*

5- Ferdinand Ludwig and Daniel Schönle, "Growing Architecture for the Planetary Garden: Position Paper on Living Architecture in the Context of Gardens and Healthy Environment," in *Landscape Architecture*, 28 (10/2021): 120-128.

Inspired by the habitat of mountain gorillas in Rwanda, Haus Daita (2019) in Tokyo, by suzuko yamada architects, blends in with its surroundings. Steel, wood and, above all, trees create an open, mutable structure in which interior and exterior spaces merge.

Biographies

ANDJELKA BADNJAR is an architect, researcher, and cocurator of the exhibition *Trees, Time, Architecture!* She has degrees from the University of Belgrade and the Politècnica de Catalunya and did her doctorate at the RWTH Aachen. She is currently working as a research associate for the Chair of History of Architecture and Curatorial Practice at the Technical University of Munich (TUM) and is a curator at its Architekturmuseum der TUM. Her areas of interest as a researcher include forms of collective building and the relationship between architecture and social theory. Her book *Praxis of Collective Building: Narratives of Philosophy and Construction* was published in 2023, and her articles have appeared in journals such as *Grey Room*, *OASE*, *Histories of Postwar Architecture*, and *North Street Review*.

JEAN-MARC CAIMI and VALENTINA PICCINNI have been collaborating since 2013 on documentary and personal photography projects. Their focus centers on contemporary subjects, with a particular emphasis on the human dimensions of each narrative. Their works are globally recognized and regularly featured in media outlets such as the *Guardian*, *Die Zeit*, *Financial Times*, *Geo*, *Der Spiegel*, *Politico*, *Le Monde*, *Libération*, *Vogue*, *L'Espresso*, *Internazionale*, *Wired*, *GQ*, *Newsweek*, the *Sunday Times*, the *Atlantic*, and numerous others. The duo has earned several awards, including the ISPA Award for best photo environmental story, the 2024 Earth Photo Award, the PhMuseum of Humanity Grant, won the Sony World Photography Award in 2019 in the "discovery" category, and were runners-up in 2024. They showcase their works in galleries and festivals such as the Biennale Für Aktuelle Fotografie, Phest, Fotodoks, and Fotografia Europea. With a portfolio of six published books, their recent releases include "Fastidiosa" and "En Présence De L'Absence," exploring themes like the Xylella plant pest in southern Italy. They've previously published a trilogy on cities in transition; *Güle Güle* received recognition at awards and competitions such as the Kassel Dummy Book Award, Prix Nadar, and was a finalist at the Arles Author Book Award. They have regularly covered events in Ukraine, producing numerous stories since the 2013 Maidan Revolution.

KELLY CHURCH is an Ottawa/Pottawatomi black ash basketmaker, fiber artist, educator, activist, and culture keeper. She comes from an unbroken line of black ash basketmakers and from the largest black ash weaving family in the Great Lakes region. Her work has been celebrated in the Chicago Field Museum, the Smithsonian Renwick Museum in Washington, DC, and the National Museum of the American Indian. She has received honors and awards, including being named a National Endowment for the Arts National Heritage Fellow, earning a Native Arts and Cultures Foundation's National Artist Fellowship, and has been a four-time Artist Leadership Program participant of the Smithsonian National Museum of the American Indian.

ZIJING DENG is a landscape architect with experience in both Asia and Europe. Her bachelor's in landscape architecture is from South China Agricultural University, 2019. Her joint research won an IFLA Asia-Pac Award of Excellence. Her master's degree in landscape architecture from TU Munich includes a thesis on the future urban space in Guangzhou, China, emphasizing humans and banyan trees as active stakeholders. She has experience in architecture and landscape architecture offices in China, The Netherlands, and Germany.

SONJA DÜMPELMANN is Professor and Chair of Environmental Humanities at Ludwig Maximilian University of Munich and a historian of urban landscapes and environments. She was previously professor in the Department of Landscape Architecture at the University of Pennsylvania Stuart Weitzman School of Design and taught for almost twenty years in the US. Her books include the award-winning *Landscapes for Sport: Histories of Physical Exercise, Sport, and Health* (2022), and *Seeing Trees: A History of Street Trees in New York City and Berlin* (2019).

ÉDOUARD FRANÇOIS is an architect, urban planner, and a graduate of the École Nationale Supérieure des Beaux-Arts in Paris. He has taught at the Architectural Association in London, the Design Academy in Eindhoven, Harvard University in the US, the ESA in Paris, the École Nationale Supérieure de Paysage in Versailles, and the Mediterranean School of Gardens and Landscape in Grasse.
In 2011, he was named Designer of the Year, and the Royal Institute of British Architects awarded him the title of International Fellow (INT.FRIBA). In 2012, he was appointed Chevalier of Arts and Letters by the French Minister of Culture. In 2016, he was elected a member of the Academy of Architecture. DOMUS magazine ranked Maison Edouard François among the 100 Best Architecture Firms in 2019. His drawings and models are part of the MNAM CCI—Centre Pompidou collections. His work is regularly exhibited at international institutions such as the Museum of Modern Art (MOMA) and Guggenheim Museum in New York, the Canadian Centre for Architecture in Montréal, the Frac Centre in Orléans, the Victoria & Albert Museum in London, and the Venice Architecture Biennale.

HANNES HARTER studied biobased products and bioenergy (BSc) at the University of Hohenheim and sustainable energy competence (MSc) at the HFT Stuttgart. On completion of his master's, he spent the years 2017 to 2022 as a research assistant at the Chair of Energy Efficient and Sustainable Design and Building (ENPB) at the Technical University of Munich (TUM), which awarded him a doctorate in 2021. He was a postdoc at the Norwegian University of Science and Technology (NTNU) in Trondheim from 2022 to 2023 and headed the department for Sustainable Neighborhoods and Cities at LIST Eco GmbH & Co. KG from 2023 to 2024. Harter is also a cofounder of vesta sustainability consulting, and since August 2024 its managing director.

SAMANTHA JAMERO is an architect in training and research assistant at the University of Maryland, College Park, where she received a M.Arch in Architecture and M.C.P. in Community Planning. She has several years of experience working in architectural practice, at the Maryland National Capital Park and Planning Commission, and for Partners for Action Learning in Sustainability (PALS) program of the National Center for Smart Growth.

SALOMÉ JASHI is a documentary filmmaker from Georgia. Her *Taming the Garden* (2021) premiered at Sundance and Berlinale Forum and was nominated for the European Film Awards. Her earlier works include *The Dazzling Light of Sunset* (2016), awarded at Visions du Réel; and *Bakhmaro* (2011), nominated for the Asia Pacific Screen Awards and Silver Eye Awards. The body of her work including features and shorts was celebrated at BAMPFA in 2023. Salomé Jashi tutors and gives talks internationally. She is chairperson and co-founder of DOCA—Documentary Association Georgia. She's a recipient of the Berlin Art Prize and the European Cultural Award KAIROS Prize (2024).

MORNINGSTAR KHONGTHAW is an environmental activist and conservationist dedicated to preserving the unique cultural heritage of Meghalaya's living root bridges. In 2017, he founded the Living Root Bridge Foundation. The foundation works to conserve these bridges, essential for daily life and tourism, by engaging local communities, especially youth, in their maintenance and knowledge preservation. Morningstar has collaborated with international institutions, including the United Nations Environment Programme and TUM, and leads sustainable tourism initiatives in his village, Rangthylliang, and the wider region.

LAURA LEONELLI is a journalist who collaborates with the cultural supplement of *Il Sole 24 Ore*, *Arte*, and *AD*. She is the curator of the Ettore Molinario Collection. She published *Siberia per due. Madre e figlia lungo lo Enisej* (Feltrinelli), *Lem. Initiation of a little Buddha* (Contrasto), *Rosalia Rabinovich. Stella rossa* (Biffi Arte), *Paolo Ventura. Autobiografia di un impostore* (Johan & Levi), and *I won't come down. Women who climb trees and look into the distance* (Postcart). For a long time she has been studying and collecting anonymous photography.

ANDRES LEPIK has been director of the Architekturmuseum of the Technical University of Munich (TUM) at the Pinakothek der Moderne and professor of History of Architecture and Curatorial Practice at the TUM since 2012. He studied history of art at the University of Augsburg and wrote his doctoral dissertation, "The Architectural Model in Italy: 1350–1500," in 1991. He was a curator at the Staatliche Museen zu Berlin as of 1994 and headed their art library's collection of twentieth- and twenty-first-century architecture from 2004 to 2007. He was curator in the Department of Architecture and Design at the Museum of Modern Art, New York, from 2007 to 2011 and was the 2011–12 Loeb Fellow at the Graduate School of Design at Harvard University. Among the most important exhibitions that he has curated are *Content/Rem Koolhaas* at the Neue Nationalgalerie, Berlin (2003), and *Small Scale, Big Change. New Architectures of Social Engagement* (2010) at MoMA. In Munich he curated *AFRITECTURE* (2013), *LINA BO BARDI 100* (2014), *Francis Kéré. Radically Simple* (2016), and *Who's Next? Homelessness, Architecture, and Cities* (2021–22). Andres Lepik is a prolific writer and editor and is the author of numerous scholarly essays, newspaper articles, and reviews on both contemporary architecture and the history of architecture.

FERDINAND LUDWIG, curator and colead of *Trees, Time, Architecture!* alongside Kristina Pujkilović, has been professor for Green Technologies in Landscape Architecture at the Technical University of Munich (TUM) since 2017 and is a partner in OLA—Office for Living Architecture. He founded Baubotanik as a research field in 2007 and has been studying and designing living architectural structures built with trees for twenty years. His book *Growing Architecture: How to Design and Build with Trees* was published by Birkhäuser in 2023. Among his research projects are the living root bridges of the Khasi, which he studied in collaboration with Dr W. Middleton; the development of Baubotanik design methods, including digital tools for factoring in growth processes; and ecological dynamics in the design process. His office has produced designs that have won international acclaim and awards, among them the Plane-Tree Cube in Nagold and the House of the Future in Berlin.

ELAHE MAHDAVI is an architectural engineering graduate from Islamic Azad University of Tehran, a master's student at TU Munich, and works at EDR GmbH. Her work focuses on sustainable architecture and urban design. She has received an Oskar von Miller Forum scholarship and TUM International Student Scholarships. Elahe has worked as an architect in Iran and Germany.

ROBERTA MARTUFI is an architect who has been dealing with topics of cultural heritage and landscape since her university education. Her work as an architect is mainly focused on restoration works of monumental assets and historic gardens. In addition, she actively researches and teaches at the universities of IUAV (University Institute of Architecture of Venice) and Carlo Bo-Urbino. Her main restoration work carried out on historic villas and gardens include Villa Almerici, Villa Caprile, Villa Ciacchi, Villa Miralfiore, Villa Montani, and Villa Vittoria, all in the territory of the ancient Duchy of Urbino. She has numerous publications on urban and landscape history, and on historic villas and gardens.

SHELBI NAHWILET MEISSNER, PhD, is an assistant professor in the Harriet Tubman Department of Women, Gender, and Sexuality Studies at University of Maryland and Director of the Indigenous Futures Lab (https://wgss.umd.edu/ifl). Meissner was recipient of the NSF and the Kaleta A. Doolin Foundation Ocean Decade Champion Award in 2023 and has expertise in Indigenous knowledge and land-based social and political philosophies.

WILFRID MIDDLETON's research explores the combination of vernacular and digital techniques in design. His work involves the use of point clouds for analyzing and designing trees in built structures and the built environment. As a post-doctoral researcher at The King's Foundation, Wilf is investigating vernacular design in Sierra Leone, Guyana, Tanzania, and India. During his PhD (TUM, 2023), he focused on Meghalaya's living root bridges, developing workflows for their analysis in terms of regenerative design, mechanics, and topology.

RICO NEWMAN is an Elder Council Member of Choptico Band, Piscataway-Conoy. He has been the director of the Maryland Indian Tourism Association for over twenty-two years and brings awareness to Yakiocanahagari, land between the Potomac and Patuxant Rivers, through the Maryland Indian Heritage Trails development. He has served as an education committee member on the Maryland Commission on Indian Affairs and worked as a Cultural Information Specialist at the Smithsonian National Museum of the American Indian for many years.

MARK PRIMACK is a Situationist who at times engages in drawing, writing, designing, building, critiquing, and politicking. He holds degrees from the Rhode Island School of Design and the Architectural Association in London. He resides in Santa Cruz, California, where he has maintained an architectural practice for forty years and has served on various commissions and the city council. In 1978 he was awarded a special projects grant from the California Arts Council to document the World Famous Tree Circus, but has supported his own work ever since. He lives, works, draws, and gardens in spaces of his own design, which he shares with landscape architect and artist Janet Pollock.

KRISTINA PUJKILOVIĆ, curator and colead of *Trees, Time, Architecture!* alongside Ferdinand Ludwig, is currently a research associate for the Chair of Green Technologies in Landscape Architecture at the Technical University of Munich (TUM). She was also a co-developer of the symposium ArchitectureNature—NatureArchitecture. Her work stands out on account of her transdisciplinary approach at the interface of landscape architecture, art, graphic design, and curatorial practice. Pujkilović studied landscape architecture at the Hochschule Weihenstephan-Triesdorf, the University of Copenhagen, and the TUM; and worked for several landscape architects and urban planners both during and after her studies.

JAKOB RAUSCHER studied architecture at the Staatliche Akademie der Bildenden Künste Stuttgart and the École Spéciale d'Architecture in Paris. He is especially interested in conceptual design and typically considers unusual parameters such as time, growth, and repurposing, and looks at tiny houses for inspiration for his solutions. He is a founding partner of OLA—Office for Living Architecture, and, as project manager at Daniel Schönle Architektur und Stadtplanung from 2012 to 2024, designed whole neighborhoods, houses, and architectural structures made of trees. From 2016 to 2019 he was a research assistant in the Principles of Local and Regional Planning department at the University of Stuttgart's Institute of Urbanism.

DANIEL SCHÖNLE studied architecture and urban planning at the University of Stuttgart and in 2003 began working on interdisciplinary teams for offices all over Germany and abroad, as well as taking part in competitions. He became a registered freelance architect and urban planner in 2008, and now runs a planning office in Stuttgart that handles projects of all sizes. Schönle is especially interested in the conceptual aspects of architecture and urbanism and is a founding partner of OLA—Office for Living Architecture. He also teaches at various institutes of higher education. He was a research assistant at the

University of Stuttgart's Institute of Urbanism from March 2010 to August 2011 and there deputized as head of Principles of Local and Regional Planning from April 2016 to September 2019.

strobo B M is a design studio that was founded in Berlin by Matthias Friederich and Julian von Klier in 2012, when the awarding of a scholarship by Olafur Eliasson and a resulting teaching position at the Institute for Spatial Experiments at Berlin University of the Arts, created the circumstances of their collaboration. The studio, which moved to Munich in 2014, specializes in the development of visual identities, editorial design, digital media, and exhibition graphics at the interface of culture, architecture, education, and research. strobo B M has won numerous national and international prizes, including the German Design Award, the International Digital Emmy Award, the Schönste Bücher Deutschlands, ADC, and the 100 Beste Plakate. It was also nominated for the City of Munich's 2022 Förderpreis für Design.

JANA VANDERGOOT, RA Architect, has twenty-five years of experience designing wood buildings. She is a tenured associate professor at University of Maryland School of Architecture, Planning, and Preservation. Her work has received US Forest Service Wood Innovations, US National Science Foundation, Chesapeake Bay Trust, and VentureWell funding. Her collaboration with members of the Piscataway Tribe and Nanticoke Nation has been recognized by an ACSA/SLB Timber Education Prize Honorable Mention. She is author of the book *Architecture and the Forest Aesthetic: A New Look at Design and Resilient Urbanism* (Routledge Press, 2018).

NOËL VAN DOOREN began his work as a landscape architect at the Dutch office of H+N+S landscape architects in 1992. He became member of the Blauwe Kamer professional magazine board in 1996, and was head of the landscape architecture program of the Amsterdam Academy of Architecture from 2004 to 2009. This led to a practice-based PhD research project hosted at the University of Amsterdam, resulting in the defence of *Drawing Time* in 2017. This work explores the representation of aspects of time in landscape architectural drawings from a historical, professional, and future perspective. Today, he acts as a strategic policy advisor on spatial affairs and conducts research on food, landscape, and agriculture. His *Drawing Time* research is continued in lectures, workshops, and essays.

MICHAEL VOLLMER studied building physics (BSc) at the HFT Stuttgart and energy efficient and sustainable building (MSc) at the Technical University of Munich (TUM). He then worked for three years as a consultant for building physics at Müller-BBM, and in 2017 took up the position of research assistant at the Chair of Energy Efficient and Sustainable Design and Building (ENPB) at the TUM. The doctorate he was awarded there in 2023 was for his development of a method for the determination and optimization of the ecological land demand of buildings based on life cycle analysis and thermal building building simulations. Vollmer is a cofounder and managing director of vesta sustainability consulting, founded in July 2020, and also works as a DGNB auditor.

WHITE ARKITEKTER is a renowned Scandinavian architecture practice founded in Gothenburg, Sweden, in 1951. Known for its commitment to sustainability and human-centered design, White has become one of the leading architectural practices in Europe, with over 700 employees working across 13 studios in Sweden, Germany, and the UK. White Arkitekter's philosophy centers on creating buildings and spaces that promote social, environmental, and economic well-being. Their projects span diverse sectors, including residential, cultural, healthcare, and urban development, often incorporating innovative approaches to energy efficiency, renewable materials, and circular design principles. Recent notable works include the Sara Cultural Centre in Skellefteå, one of the world's tallest timber buildings, and their extensive contributions to urban renewal projects in cities throughout Scandinavia. Through a mix of tradition with contemporary analysis, White Arkitekter continues to inspire sustainable architecture globally, aiming for all projects to be climate-neutral by 2030.

Image credits

Ferdinand Ludwig and Kristina Pujkilović:
p. 10 Fig 1: © Photo: Duncan Lewis Scape Architecture, Cornebarrieu 2005
p. 12 Fig 2: © Photo: Daniela Valentini, Zurich, 2008
p. 12 Fig 3: © TUM, Photo: Ferdinand Ludwig, 2019
pp. 16–17 Fig 4:
© Photo: Roman Mensing Fotografie, Eicherscheid, 2021, www.romanmensing.de

Sonja Dümpelmann:
p. 18 Fig 1: Bayerische Staatsbibliothek München, Oecon. 663 q-81
p. 21 Fig 3: Bayerische Staatsbibliothek München, Oecon. 1209

Noël van Dooren:
p. 28 Fig 1: Courtesy of MTD Landschapsarchitecten, Den Bosch, The Netherlands
p. 31 Fig 2: Courtesy of Lawrence Halprin Collection, the Architectural Archives, University of Pennsylvania
p. 32 Fig 3: Courtesy of Roland Gustavsson, Alnarp, Sweden
p. 32 Fig 4: Courtesy of Anouk Vogel, Amsterdam, The Netherlands

p. 33 Fig 5: Drawings collection of Danish National Art Library, 53182a, Udstykning fra Højstrupgård, haveanlæg 1948–1950 for DAB
p. 34 Fig 6: Courtesy of Michel Desvigne Paysagiste, Paris, France
p. 34 Fig 7: Courtesy of Johanna Bendlin, Brussels, Belgium
p. 35 Fig 8: Courtesy of Atelier Le Balto, Berlin, Germany

Jana VanderGoot:
p. 38 Fig 1: https://www.thecanadianencyclopedia.ca/en/article/snow-shoes.
p. 41 Fig 4: © Zeynep Demircan
p. 41 Fig 5: © Jana VanderGoot, 2023
pp. 42–43
Figs 6, 7: Smithsonian National Museum of the American Indian Cultural Resources Center

Morningstar Khongthaw and Wilfrid Middleton in Conversation with Kristina Pujkilović:
pp. 62, 65, 68–69
© TUM, Photo: Ferdinand Ludwig, India, 2019

Wilfrid Middleton, Zijing Deng, Elahe Mahdavi, and Ferdinand Ludwig:
p. 75 Fig 7: © Photo: Swastik Mazumder

Mark Primack:
p. 80 Fig 7: © Photo: Tony Grant
p. 81 Fig 11: © Photo: Gypsy Ray
p. 82 Fig 12: © Photo: Joel Leivick

Édouard François:
p. 86 Fig 1: © Photo Pierre L'Excellent
p. 88 Fig 3: Centre G. Pompidou collection
p. 91 Fig 7: FRAC Centre-Val de Loire collection

Roberta Martufi:
p. 92 Fig 1: ga Khan Museum, Toronto
p. 94 Fig 2: https://commons.wikimedia.org/wiki/File:Saint_Simeon_and_Saint_David.jpg
p. 94 Fig 4: Courtesy Ministero della Cultura – Musei nazionali di Bologna
p. 95 Fig 5: Istituto centrale per la digitalizzazione del patrimonio culturale
p. 95 Fig 6: The Elisha Whittelsey Collection, The Met, New York
p. 95 Fig 7: Herzogin Anna Amalia Bibliothek, Klassik Stiftung Weimar
p. 96 Fig 8: Münchener DigitalisierungsZentrum (MDZ)
p. 97 Fig 9: Photo Archive of Civica Pinacoteca il Guercino di Cento

p. 99 Fig 10: © Photo: David Scarle
p. 99 Fig 11: Getty Research Institute, https://catalog.hathitrust.org/Record/008695983
p. 99 Fig 12: private collection
p. 99 Fig 13: © Photo: Ji-Elle

Salomé Jashi:
All images are stills from the documentary *Taming the Garden*, R: Salomé Jashi, Mira Film / Corso Film / Sakdoc Film, 2021.
pp. 100, 106–108
Figs 1–3, 6–8, 10, 11: Shot cinematographer: Salomé Jashi
pp. 107–109
Figs 4, 5, 9, 12–14: Shot cinematographer: Goga Devdariani

Hannes Harter and Michael Vollmer in Conversation with Ferdinand Ludwig and Kristina Pujkilović:
pp. 110 and 115:
© White Arkitekter
p. 113: © GOA Architecture

Ferdinand Ludwig, Daniel Schönle, and Jakob Rauscher:
p. 116: © BIOCOM AG
pp. 119 and 120: © OLA

p. 122: © suzuko yamada architects, photo: Kei Sasaki, 2019

Cover © strobo B M, 2025
Inside Cover: Detail image from the augmented reality model of the root bridge in Nongbareh, Meghalaya, India. © Marco Pisano, Wilfrid Middleton, 2025

Imprint

The catalog is published on the occasion of the exhibition
Trees, Time, Architecture! Design in Constant Transformation.

Architekturmuseum der TUM at the Pinakothek der Moderne Munich, 13.03.→14.09.2025

Editors: Andjelka Badnjar, Kristina Pujkilović, Ferdinand Ludwig, Andres Lepik
Translations: Bronwen Saunders, Elaine Hardy, Lumi Kirk, Sandra Persiani
Copy editing: Christen Jamar
Proofreading: Charlotte Eckler
Graphic design: strobo B M (Matthias Friederich, Julian von Klier, Sabrina Baumann)
Image processing, printing, and binding: gugler* DruckSinn, Melk, Österreich

© 2025 Andjelka Badnjar, Kristina Pujkilović, Ferdinand Ludwig, Andres Lepik, and Park Books AG, Zurich
© for the texts: the authors
© for the images: the artists / see image credits, p. 127

Park Books
Niederdorfstrasse 54
8001 Zurich
Switzerland
www.park-books.com
T +41 44 262 16 62
E info@park-books.com

Product safety
Responsible person pursuant to EU Regulation 2023/988 (GPSR):
GVA Gemeinsame Verlagsauslieferung Göttingen GmbH & Co. KG
Post Box 2021
37010 Göttingen
Germany
T +49 551 384 200 0
E info@gva-verlage.de

Park Books is being supported by the Federal Office of Culture with a general subsidy for the years 2021–2025.

All rights reserved; no part of this publication may be reproduced, stored in a retrieval system or transmitted in any form or by any means, electronic, mechanical, photocopying, recording, or otherwise, without the prior written consent of the publisher.

ISBN 978-3-03860-431-0

EXHIBITION
Director: Andres Lepik
Head of project / Curatorial lead: Ferdinand Ludwig, Kristina Pujkilović
Co-Curation: Andjelka Badnjar Gojnić
Project coordination: Andres Lepik
Scientific and curatorial advisory board: Noël van Dooren, Sonja Dümpelmann
Student assistants: Maximilian Atta, Chang Chen, Philipp Endisch, Günter Georg Merk, Amelie Steffen, Pauline Wessel, Felix Zimmermann, Yi Zhou
Exhibition design: Buero Kofink Schels (Simon Jüttner, Sebastian Kofink, Tobias Trübenbacher)
Graphic design: strobo B M (Matthias Friederich, Julian von Klier, Sabrina Baumann)
Interaction design: Marco Pisano
Vegetation technology: Christoph Fleckenstein
Copy editing and Translations: Lumi Kirk
Coordination of the public program: Dietlind Bachmeier and Ulrich Ball
Technical exhibition planning and execution: Andreas Bohmann, Volker Enders, Thomas Lohmaier
Conservator: Anton Heine
Registrar: Thilo Schuster

Secretariat: Martina Heinemann, Rosa Anna Perrini, Rike Menacher, Aigerim Shakanova
Public relations: Martina Heinemann, Lisa Clausen-Schaumann
Press: Cara Hähl-Pfeifer, Tine Nehler, Julia Kaufmann
Children workshops: Enrica Ferrucci
Printed matter: ESCHER Digitaldruck

Funded by the German Federal Cultural Foundation

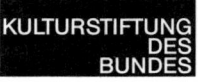

Funded by the Federal Government Comissioner for Culture and the Media

 Die Beauftragte der Bundesregierung für Kultur und Medien

PIN. Freunde der Pinakothek der Moderne e.V.

Technische Universität München

ACKNOWLEDGMENTS
The curators would like to express their sincere thanks to all architects, designers, artists, colleagues at TUM, lenders, and students who contributed to the success of the exhibition and the catalogue.

Special thanks go to:
Lukas Allner, Sandra Bartoli, Carson Chan, Gilles Clement, Ines Dantas, Christoph Fleckenstein, Philipp Gruber, Cornelius Hackenbracht, Ilkka Halso, Guido Jost, Morningstar Khongthaw, Shiningstar Khongthaw, Mangkyrpang Khongdup, Christoph Kaltenbrunner, Daniela Kröhnert, Lea Kuttkat, Jana Langner, Laura Leonelli, Duncan Lewis, Wilhelm Ley GmbH, Slivan Linden, Felix Lüdicke, Roman Mensing, Wilfrid Middleton, Anna Oelsner, Dominik Ophey, Mark Primack, Jakob Rauscher, Chris Reding, Julia Roemer, SANlight GmbH, Darleen Schäfer, Singer Regale & Hallenbau GmbH, Daniel Schönle, Bernhard Schöner, Lukretia Weeth, White Arkitekter